HEREAFTER

Also by Richard Schweid

Che's Chevrolet, Fidel's Oldsmobile:
On the Road in Cuba

Consider the Eel:
A Natural and Gastronomic History

The Cockroach Papers:
A Compendium of History and Lore

Hot Peppers:
The Story of Cajuns and Capsicum

The Catfish and the Delta:
Confederate Fish Farming in the Mississippi Delta

HEREAFTER

Searching for Immorality

RICHARD SCHWEID

THUNDER'S MOUTH PRESS
NEW YORK

HEREAFTER: *Searching for Immortality*

Published by
Thunder's Mouth Press
An Imprint of Avalon Publishing Group, Inc.
245 West 17th Street, 11th floor
New York, NY 10011

AVALON
publishing group incorporated

First printing, August 2006

Library of Congress Cataloging-in-Publication Data is available.

ISBN-10: 1-56025-657-5
ISBN-13: 978-1-56025-657-1

9 8 7 6 5 4 3 2 1

Book design by Maria E. Torres

Printed in the United States of America
Distributed by Publishers Group West

For Michael Golden—may he long be among the living;
we've got plenty of time to be dead

And to the memory of those family and friends who died
while I was working on this book:
Adele Mills Schweid, Kay Stoddard, and Marty Jezer.

CONTENTS

Visankharagatam cittam,

Gone to dissolution is the mind,

Tanhanam khayam ajjhaga.

The cravings have come to an end.

—from the Buddha's "Hymn to Victory" (sixth century BCE)

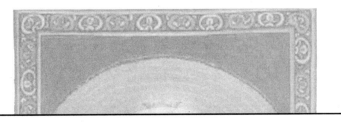

PART ONE
Body and Soul

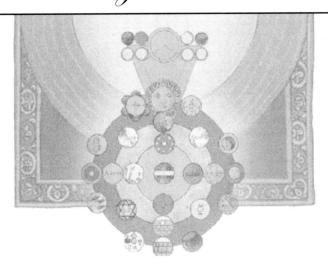

The heart of a dead person is weighed against a feather. *Courtesy of Alexandre Caron, iStockphoto.*

Going Forth by Day

There is none who comes back from there,
That he may tell their state,
That he may tell their needs,
That he may still our hearts,
Until we may travel to the place where they have gone.

From "Song of the Harper,"
Egyptian poem, circa twenty-first century BCE,
as quoted in *The Judgement of the Dead*, by S. G. F. Brandon

As long as people have been on earth, they have constructed various interpretations and explanations of what happens after death. Other than our physical forms, our genetic structures, and our most basic behaviors, we have little in common with our earliest ancestors in terms of how we live our day-to-day lives. One thing we do share across the ages is our helplessness in the face of the fact that this self, which takes so much effort to construct and inhabit and nurture, this body that we've worn and washed and lived in, is likely to last considerably less than a century. While we live longer than Cro-Magnon man, and presumably better, we are as much at the mercy of an individual demise as ever. All of the memories and learning and love that we have so painstakingly accumulated, each in our own lives, is destined to be wiped out in a moment.

Humans have responded over the centuries to this inescapable fact, in one of three basic ways: some believe that somehow we shall be resurrected to pass eternity with intact bodies as the same people we were during our earthly sojourns; others believe that what survives death is a "soul," or an essence, which leaves behind forever the dead and decomposing physical body in which it resided to move on in some fashion; and still others believe that death melts our snowflake lives entirely. Of course, a sizeable number of people profess simply not to know what happens when we die, but those who reached a conclusion, across the millennia, fell into one of those three groups.

The written record regarding immortality goes back to Egypt and Persia nearly five thousand years ago, but we can be certain that a yearning for immortality goes back much further than that, back to the first people on earth, the first death, the first grief over a loved one's sudden and permanent transformation from animate to inanimate. As long as people have died, since the beginning of human time, people have imagined immortality, they have elaborated explanations of why we die, and they have constructed belief systems about the afterlife—eschatologies—around these things.

Approximately 100 billion people have lived since the end of the most recent ice age, according to researchers. One hundred billion. They have also died, every last one of them, and none has come back to talk about it. Each of those 100 billion lives extinguished is an abrupt separation from family and the world. Death took them at various stages in their lives, and in a multitude of ways, but take them it did. Death humbles us individually and as a species. For all our higher brains and larger imposition on the earth's resources, we share with the humblest spider, the merest mite, and blindest earthworm a common destiny. Death came in one of many different forms to each of those 100 billion people, but whether a last breath was drawn in a body ravaged and exhausted by cancer or felled in the moment by an aneurysm, killed in battle or suddenly dead in the crib, the same thing happened to their bodies when they died. They decayed, rapidly at first, then more slowly, until finally only bones and teeth remained. The body's putrefaction is inevitable and indisputable, and most people will acknowledge that this is so. Yet millions are convinced that the power of God and their faith in that power is enough miraculously to overcome death's physical consequences and that they will pass eternity in resurrected bodies.

This belief is generally held by the more fundamentalist faithful, who envision a hereafter in which our forms, memories, and personalities remain. It will certainly require a miracle, given what we know for certain about the failures of the flesh, about what happens to our bodies when we die. Once our blood has stopped flowing and nourishment ceases to arrive to feed our cells, the proteins that have powered us have no recourse but to feed on the flesh around them and devour us from the inside out. The body consumes itself. The details, mostly bacterial, liquid, and evil smelling, are not pretty, but they are worth bearing in mind when considering the notion of physical immortality, the belief that this process can be miraculously reversed or that our likenesses can be recovered at a later date. The body's disintegration is succinctly described by Heather Pringle in her book, *The Mummy Congress.*

"Within days [of death], the epidermis loses its waxy pallor. It turns a delicate shade of green, then purple, finally black. The face, scrotum, and vulva swell and the abdomen bloats. In some cases, the body puffs up like a balloon to three times its normal size. Then it cracks open like a cocoon. A bloody ooze trickles from the nose and mouth." Eyeballs liquefy. Blisters bubble along the skin and burst.

None of that has happened yet to the corpse on the table in front of me, about to be cut open on an April morning in 2005. I have never watched an autopsy and I can count on one hand the number of whole dead bodies I have seen in sixty years, even when I include funerals. I don't much like the sight of blood and bone, although up until now, the few times I have had to bear it, at least I did not faint. That could be about to change, I figure, but it seems like a good idea when considering bodily resurrection to know, at least, what the inside of a body actually looks like.

Charles Harlan, a freelance pathologist and former county coroner in Nashville, Tennessee, says he often does three or four autopsies a week to deduce why someone has died, and estimates he has done at least twenty thousand in his lifetime, including one on the body of Elvis Presley ("heart attack"). He is fifty-seven years old, has short, white hair brushed back, a florid round face with a pair of sizable bifocals in front of alert brown eyes, and a body shaped like a pear. He is stout and red-faced, wearing dark-blue, short-sleeve medical scrubs, and his pale forearms look strong. He is not a tall man but has large hands, and before he dons his latex gloves, I see that his fingernails are trimmed and immaculately clean.

His job today is straightforward: to determine the cause of death for the fifteen-year-old white male on the stainless steel table in the room where Harlan works. He has looked at X-rays of the dead boy's chest and has already formed an opinion—congestive respiratory and heart failure brought on by viral pneumonia. The autopsy will confirm or disprove this hypothesis. His place of business is located in a strip of warehouses and low, one-story factories in an industrial Nashville neighborhood down by the Cumberland River. The back of the building is a large garage where a hearse can easily be unloaded. The autopsy room is low with walls of cheap wood paneling. A long neon tube above the table on a water-stained Styrofoam ceiling provides the light. It looks more like a room in a house trailer than a medical environment, until one takes into account the spotless table and the gleaming instruments laid out on a counter. The table has a drain at one end, between the corpse's feet, connected by a drainpipe to a sink behind it.

The boy's dead body was discovered by his mother eighteen hours ago, lying on the floor of his bedroom. While it still looks lifelike, the corpse is already showing some signs that it is no longer a functioning machine. I gingerly touch a forearm. The skin is ice cold. Both plethora and rigor mortis have set in—the former is the pooling of blood in places like the buttocks, back, and upper arms, turning the skin a mottled violet; the latter, the stiffening up of joints, meaning the corpse has lost flexibility.

The dead boy's mother and sister were out shopping and returned home in midafternoon to make the terrible discovery. He was a nice-looking young guy, five feet ten inches tall, 182 pounds, short, sandy hair, well-shaped face and body, muscular and trim, flat belly, hairless to his pubis where a circumcised penis lies limp in an abundant thatch of ginger hair. A boy whose sudden death would wound a mother to her core. The question the Franklin County

Sheriff's Office wants answered, and the reason to pay for a deputy to drive the corpse in a hearse to Nashville, is to find out exactly why the boy died. His mother said he was suffering from allergies but that nothing else was wrong. It is a pathologist's job in such cases to open the body, take out and weigh the organs, and inspect them to determine the cause of death. Autopsy comes from the Greek word, *autopsia*, meaning "seeing with one's own eyes" and that will be Harlan's job today.

I'm much closer to the stainless steel table than I had anticipated. In my mind, I had imagined I would be seated above an operating theater looking down on the proceedings at a safe remove. I was way wrong. Carolyn Harlan, wife, office manager, and pathology assistant seats me on a barstool less than a yard from the dead kid's handsome head. I ask her for directions to the bathroom in case I have to rush away and vomit. She hands me a cotton surgical mask that loops over my ears and covers my nose. "You may want to wear this when we get him opened up. We're used to it, but the smell can be pretty strong if it's your first time."

I sniff the air. Nothing yet. Harlan unties the rag from around the boy's wrists that has been holding his hands together on his belly, so that they would not flop around on the ride in from Franklin County. "The first thing I have to do is break the rigor mortis," he tells me, snapping the arms upward, suddenly, then laying them along the corpse's sides.

An autopsy is as much a medical procedure as is an

appendectomy or brain surgery. Once the arms are positioned and the hands are out of the way, Harlan gets to work.
A hard plastic chock is positioned under the kid's back, which
pushes his chest up in the air for easy access, while his head
lolls back on the table, tongue protruding enough to cover
his lower lip, dead eyes slightly open. A pathologist begins an
autopsy by making a Y incision with a scalpel, beginning in
the middle of each shoulder, around the outside of each
nipple to dovetail below the breastbone and run in a single
line down to the pelvis. The flesh over the rib cage is cut away
with a broad-blade knife and peeled back toward the face, a
big swatch of skin on top of three-quarters of an inch of
yellow fat over pink-and-red muscle. Yellows, purples, and
reds are the colors under the poor kid's skin, as they are under
yours and mine and every other mortal's. "This knife was
given to me by my mentor, whose students gave it to him,"
Harlan said, as he folded back the flesh like a carpet.

The next step is to cut through the rib cage, taking out a
shield-shaped piece and opening up the peritoneal cavity.
He uses a Stryker saw—a small, round blade on a thick
handle, which a person can bear down on. The chest opens
easily. No blood comes spurting out, because the heart is no
longer pumping, but—whoa—a smell rises in the narrow
room, it fills the air as the top of the rib cage is removed, a
penetrating bouquet of raw liver and feces. I pull the surgical mask out of my pocket and put it on. It helps a little.

Then it is on to the organs, cutting them loose and
lifting them out to put them in a plastic tray at his side.

Harlan has an assistant, introduced to me as J.J., who is also white-haired. He has a clipped white mustache and a stained smock and steps outside the room to smoke whenever his services are not required during the procedure. As Harlan takes out the organs, J.J. stands across from him, dipping a stainless steel soup ladle into the body cavity, scooping out blood, and pouring it into the drain between the corpse's feet.

All the organs are larger than I imagined; it's hard to grasp the idea of all that meaty machinery packed inside our rib cages. The boy's heart is big, and his liver looks huge, nestled up against his rib cage. The lungs, too, seem amazingly large to fit inside a chest. They are even bigger than normal, Harlan says, which points to further proof of congestive failure. He nicks the left kidney with a scalpel when he takes it out so as to differentiate it from the right one later on. Then he reaches down under the pubis to cut the bladder and prostate loose.

With all of the organs harvested, it is on to the brain. He rolls the corpse slightly to one side of the table and takes out the plastic block, which he replaces under the kid's head, tilting it upright. He cuts from behind one ear to behind the other with a scalpel. "You do it behind the ear so that the incision won't be visible when he's lying in a casket. I always try to make things easy on the funeral home."

Once he has a slice from ear to ear, he peels the scalp up toward the face with a sound like ripping cloth; the hair on top makes it look as if he's tearing a piece of turf from a lawn. He cuts and peels, cuts and peels, revealing more and more of the skull. When it is exposed, he uses the Stryker saw to open it, cutting through a quarter inch of bone, skull dust from the whirring saw blade obscuring the doctor for a moment at his grim work under the fluorescent light. How hard the skull is, how well designed to protect the delicate brain beneath. He lifts off a cap of skull to reveal the brain cupped and nestled beneath, flesh-colored and veined.

All the organs he has removed will be weighed in the second part of the autopsy. He has a hanging scale, a stainless steel basket hanging over the autopsy table, and sits across from it. He takes each organ one by one, weighs it, and calls out the numbers to Carolyn, who writes them down. He has a white plastic cutting board on the table in front of him and cuts a thin slice off each organ with a scalpel. The rest of the organ goes in a plastic tub, which is also lined with plastic. He drops the tissue samples into plastic bottles containing formaldehyde. These will be fixed and examined.

It all takes nearly three hours and will not be complete until the tissue samples are analyzed and the paperwork is done. Then Franklin County will have its autopsy results, at a cost of $750. The same service at a private hospital would cost about $1,500. The state medical examiner in Nashville charges $2,500, according to Carolyn Harlan. The savings that Charles Harlan's autopsies represent are, without a doubt, one of the reasons a number of the state's counties frequently use him instead of the public medical examiner.

❧

Getting paid for being able to divide and cleanly carve a human corpse stretches from that table in Charles Harlan's autopsy room, or the basement embalming room of any twenty-first-century funeral home, all the way back to Egyptian embalmers thousands of years ago preparing a dead body for the millennia ahead. The Egyptian was likely to have done a much better job than any contemporary undertaker could dream of, even with the high-tech tools and chemical-soup embalming fluids that modern mortuaries have at their disposal.

When the Greek historian Herodotus reported the technique from Egypt around 450 BCE, the preparation of a dead body was a science that had already been practiced for more than two thousand years. In Herodotus's day, Egyptians paying for the embalming of a loved one had three possibilities, depending on what they could afford. A dead family member needs dealing with, and an Egyptian embalmer in 450 BCE no doubt detailed the available options to a grieving family, ranging from the most expensive to the most ordinary, in a scene still played out today by morticians and clergy around the world. Those Egyptians for whom price was no object gave over their dead loved ones to an exquisite care and preparation. The goal was to leave the envelope intact, the body ready and waiting to be inhabited once again by the spirit. Not surprisingly, the most expensive turned out to be the most effective.

Herodotus revealed to his Greek readers back home how it was done.

"There are a set of men in Egypt who practice the art of embalming, and make it their proper business. . . . The mode of embalming, according to the most perfect process, is the following: They take first a crooked piece of iron, and with it draw out the brain through the nostrils, thus getting rid of a portion, while the skull is cleared of the rest by rinsing with drugs; next they make a cut along the flank with a sharp Ethiopian stone and take out the whole contents of the abdomen, which they then cleanse, washing it thoroughly with palm wine, and again frequently with an infusion of pounded aromatics. After this they fill the cavity with the purest bruised myrrh, with cassia, and every other sort of spicery except frankincense, and sew up the opening. Then the body is placed in natrum for seventy days and covered entirely over. After the expiration of that space of time, which must not be exceeded, the body is washed, and wrapped round, from head to foot, with bandages of fine linen cloth, smeared over with gum, which is generally used by the Egyptians in place of glue, and in this state it is given back to the relations, who enclose it in a wooden case which they have made for the purpose, shaped into the figure of a man. Then fastening the case, they place it in a sepulchral chamber, upright against the wall. Such is the most costly way of embalming the dead."

E. A. Wallis Budge asserted in his 1899 book, *Egyptian Ideas of the Future Life*, that the ancient Egyptians knew, after some three thousand years of practice, that most of their mummies would not last the duration. The evidence, he wrote, is incontrovertible that the educated Egyptians knew the physical body would not be resurrected, that it was vulnerable to destruction by damp, dry rot, or some other kind of decay. They were well aware, wrote Budge, that "by no human means could that which is corruptible by nature be made to become incorruptible."

However, if the Egyptians were so sure of the all-too-mortal-ness of the flesh, why did they spend large sums of money to embalm their dead? Despite the wealth of written material about death left on the walls of tombs and on papyri, Egyptologists have never clearly established what the presence of a mummified body in a tomb meant to the ancient civilization. Whatever it was, Budge insisted that the wealthy, the well-educated, and the priests all believed the physical body stayed in the tomb. But, he wrote, it also seems certain that a class of Egyptians existed who believed in literal physical resurrection. "There were ignorant people in Egypt who, no doubt, believed in the resurrection of the corruptible body, and who imagined that the new life would be, after all, something very much like a continuation of that which they were living in this world.

Whatever their ideas about the eventual fate of the body, all Egyptians seem to have believed in the continuity of life. "The Egyptians were essentially ritual optimists, believing fervently in the 'resurrection' of the dead as an individualized [*sic*] embodied self, with the whole purpose and point of the funeral rite being to rejoin the ba (soul) with the body," wrote Jon Davies in *Death, Burial and Rebirth in the Religions of Antiquity.* "The point of the funeral was to accomplish the 'going out into the day,' the new life with Osiris and as Osiris, in the delights of eternity."

Mummification is an essential part of this process, and what those who could not afford it thought would happened to their bodies is not wholly clear. Those who had the money would be prepared by the experts in the arts of death, their bodies would wait patiently for their soul to make their appointed rounds. The body waits, preserved, prepared for resurrection. The experts did good work.

Three thousand years is a long time, but much of what they prepared to last for the ages has done so, right up until now, although the withered, leathered, waxy skin of the uncorrupted arouses little envy. We know a great deal about the Egyptians—the details of their daily lives, their profound and complex religious beliefs, their funeral ceremonies, and their cosmology. For all of that knowledge, however, we have not deciphered exactly what they thought awaited after death; we are not certain how they would have described the details of the afterlife. We can, however, deduce that they believed the spirit of a person lived forever and that the physical body was not finished at death, that it played some sort of important role and needed to be maintained.

Their idea that some form of physical life continues after death may be partially rooted in the earliest Egyptians discovering that corpses were preserved when buried in sandy graves in the desert. Their burial remains reveal the dead interred in shallow pits in the sand, their bodies arranged in a fetal position. Buried in sand, a body will desiccate at a rapid pace, its liquids drawn out into the dryness around it, leaving a corpse as dry as a dead leaf. Many of these graves have yielded physical remains that have well-preserved skin and hair, according to A. J. Spencer in *Death in Ancient Egypt.* He wrote:

> This natural preservation must have been observed by the Egyptians, themselves, as, even before the appearance of tomb-robbers, burials would have been exposed by erosion or by animals, as well as by the accidental cutting of a new grave into an older one. It may be that seeing the still-lifelike bodies of the dead was the origin of the Egyptian belief in a continued existence in which survival depended upon the preservation of the body in a recognizable form. . . . Without the body the spirit had no place to rest and consequently could not exist.

What is certain is that the Egyptians expected a postmortem existence, and it would be determined by a judgment following death in which their lives and deeds would be scrutinized. A pyramid text dating from around 2500 BCE shows the scene: a dead soul being judged, with the heart of the dead person in a pan on one side of the balance, and a feather in the other. The feather was *Maat;* it represented a female goddess, a daughter of the sun god Ra (Re). *Maat* also represented a correct life, in harmony with the cosmic order and organization, the gears of the world turning smoothly. *Maat* was the principle, the spirit, of a well-ordered personal or collective life. Against it was judged the heart of a dead person, the sum of the deceased's deeds. If the heart and the feather balanced the scales, the dead person was deemed worthy to meet Osiris in the afterlife. If, however, the heart was heavier than the feather, the idea seems to have been that the sinner's soul would pass though a period in hell, with every bit as much fire and brimstone to suffer through as a sinner judged by a fundamentalist Baptist. However, the Egyptians seem to have held fast to the idea that eventually all would reach paradise, even those who would have to pass first through long periods of perdition. Over the centuries, the idea of a postmortem judgment gathered force, and by the New Kingdom, beginning around 1500 BCE, it had gained widespread acceptance. Religious writings were gathered together in what we call *The Egyptian Book of the Dead*, and which its writers called *The Book of Going Forth* by Day. The title means that the spells contained in the book are capable of giving someone the power to live during the day and not just wander at night like ghosts and spirits, according to Alan Segal in *Life After Death*. He quotes chapter 12 of *The Book of Going Forth by Day* as an example of what an Egyptian wanted to be able to say when facing judgment:

I have not done that which the gods abominate.

I have not defamed a slave to his superior.

I have not made [anyone] sick.

I have not made [anyone] weep.

I have not killed.

I have given no order to a killer.

I have not caused anyone suffering.

I have not cut down on the food in the temples,

I have not damaged the bread of the gods.

I have not taken the loaves of the blessed [dead].

I have not had sexual relations with a boy.

I have not defiled myself.

It was not only in Egypt that the idea of judgment after death was developing. At the same time as the New Kingdom period in Egypt, another great ancient religion, Zoroastrianism, was spreading rapidly across the Persian empire to the east. It had a well-defined belief in an afterlife and an individual, physical resurrection. Over the centuries, it spread across what we now know as Iran and Afghanistan. It is the oldest monotheistic religion in written history, and it is still practiced today. The tenets of Zoroastrianism were announced by the prophet Zarathustra. No one is sure when it was that Zarathustra carried the word to his people. Some sources say as far back as 1400 BCE, while others say 800 or 700 BCE.

"Zoroastrianism was already old when it first enters

recorded history," according to Mary Boyce in her book *Zoroastrians: Their Religious Beliefs and Practices.* "It has its roots in a very distant past . . . originating over 3,500 years ago in a Bronze Age culture on the Asian steppes."

It is a monotheism situated in a world seen in starkly dualistic terms, in which a supreme being named Ahura Mazda is at everlasting war with evil in the form of Angra Mainyu, later known as Ahriman. The struggle between them is played out by humanity, and it is the duty of each person to serve the good. In the end times, when Ahura Mazda, or Ormazd, as he also came to be called, finally wins, those who served him will be rewarded with eternal life.

Like the monotheisms that would follow—Judaism, Christianity, and Islam—it is an end-times religion, it prophesies a final judgment and a resurrection in the body. The Zoroastrian belief system has a surprising number of extremely close parallels with Christian thought, and some of the most basic and fundamental tenets of Christianity made their first appearances as part of it. The eternal fight of good against evil, which will end with victory for the one God, was a basic tenet of Zoroastrianism many centuries before Christianity appeared.

Nor is it difficult to find Zoroastrian references in Judaism. The first Zoroastrians left the bodies of their dead on rock outcroppings to be devoured by wild animals, but since at least the fifth century BCE, and perhaps much further back, Zoroastrians did not bury or burn their dead but rather left their bodies in a special open tower called the Tower of Silence, where they were devoured by vultures and predators. When only bones remained, they were collected and held against that day when once again the righteous would put on their new flesh and walk about. It calls to mind the biblical vision of Ezekiel 37:1–10 "The hand of the Lord was upon me, and carried me out in the spirit of the Lord, and set me down in the midst of the valley which was full of bones.

"And caused me to pass by them round about; and, behold, there were very many in the open valley; and, lo, they were very dry. . . . There was a noise, and behold a shaking, and the bones came together, bone to his bone. . . . Lo, the sinews and the flesh came upon them, and the skin covered them above. . . . And the breath came into them and they lived and stood upon their feet, an exceeding great army."

Nothing in Zoroastrianism is more impure than death, and dead Zoroastrians were borne to the Tower of Silence by those in the priestly class. Corpses were considered agents of pollution, and the uninitiated were warned to keep away from them. Herodotus, that great Greek chronicler of the wider world, reported in the fifth century BCE that their beliefs were not like those of his readers back home: "It is not customary among Persians to have idols made and temples built and altars erected. They even consider the use of them a sign of folly. They do not believe that the gods are like men, as the Greeks do."

In 586 BCE, the independent kingdom of Judah was conquered by the Babylonians, and the Jews were sent into exile. In relatively short order, the Babylonians were conquered by the Persians about 500 BC, and the Jews, like everyone else in the Middle East, were ruled from what is now Iran. It is perfectly conceivable that parts of these foreign religions made their way back to Israel and into Jewish doctrine.

Zoroastrianism had a vast body of sacred literature, the earliest book of which is the Avesta. The oldest part of the Avesta is the Gathas, which were written by Zarathustra in what is called Gathic Avestan, one of the most ancient Indo-European languages. "The Gathas contain the teachings of the Prophet about good and evil, righteousness and truth, social justice and right action," Hannah M. G. Shapero has written. "There is very little cosmology or mythology in the Gathas, but there is a sublime theology and a resounding statement of belief in the one God, Ahura Mazda, the Wise Lord."

The scant written material that has come down to us through the ages is only a small part of what was a rich literary tradition. The main body of work is thought to have been destroyed when Alexander burned the library at Persepolis during his conquest of the Persian empire in 330 BCE. The priests' oral tradition kept the texts alive in memory, and during the Sassanian era, from 250 to 650 CE, when Zoroastrianism was once again the Persian state religion, the high priests gathered the surviving texts and wrote down the oral traditions in the twenty-one volumes of the Avesta, treating a wide range of subjects, including medicine, history, and science. However, much of this body of written work created over four centuries was also destroyed by invaders, in this case the Islamic Arab invasion of Iran in the seventh century, when great numbers of books are said to have been burned.

Zoroastrians continued producing religious literature during the Middle Ages, and it was then that much of what we have today was written. In the twelfth century, under the domination of Mongolian conquerors who became Muslims, both Zoroastrians and their literature suffered great depredation. The believers who survived were a greatly reduced and scattered population, and the only writings they rescued intact were on religion and some legal texts. Among these was the Bundahishn, a part of the Zoroastrian canon. It was written down in the ninth century, according to Zoroastrian scholar Mary Boyce, who described it as the learning of ancient Iran as it evolved and was transmitted by generations of priestly schools. In chapter 30, Ormazd explains the relative ease of resurrecting the dead compared to creating the living:

When by me a son was created and fashioned in the womb of a mother, and the structure severally of the skin, nails, blood, feet, eyes, ears, and other things was produced; when by me the legs were created for the water so that it flows away, and the cloud was created that carries the water of the world and rains there where it has a purpose; when by me the air was created which conveys in one's eyesight, through the strength of the wind, the lowermost upwards according to its will, and one is not able to grasp it with the hand out-stretched; each one of them, when treated by me, was herein more difficult than causing the resurrection, for it is an assistance to me in the resurrection that they exist, but when they were formed it was not forming the future out of the past.

The Middle Ages period in which the Bundahishn was written proved to be Zoroastrianism's high point in terms of popularity. From those times forward, the number of believers shrank in the face of an increasingly strong Islam and a global dispersion of Zarathustra's followers. Over the past thirteen hundred years, the ranks of Zoroastrians in the world have shrunk while those of Muslims have swelled. Islam is an immediate and liveable religion; it is a practical and daily matter, with a strong appeal and a vivid promise of eternal paradise, often backed up over the centuries by the sword, and a promise of hell in both the afterlife and this one. The 1979 revolution of the ayatollahs in Iran—the wresting away of ancient Persia from the hands of a cosmopolitan, wealthy, Westernized ruler, returning the country to the firm administration of Islamic law—was only the latest incident in a millennia-old turning struggle in Persian and Iranian history.

Another factor contributing to the decline in numbers of Zoroastrians is that believers are born, not made. Traditionally, Zoroastrianism does not accept converts, and when a Zoroastrian contracted marriage to someone outside the faith, it meant the loss of a congregant. Even so, some 140,000 Zoroastrians around the world still practice the faith. Ten thousand are estimated to be doing so in North America, along with 4,000 in England, 45,000 in Iran, and 75,000 in India, where they are known as Parsees.

North American Zoroastrians do not leave the bodies of the dead outside to decompose or be devoured but rather cremate them. "Death pollutes, and we should not pollute," said Farang Mehr, a Zoroastrian who lives outside Boston. "We are guardians of God in this world. We benefit from the world's things and we must keep them in good shape. It's better to dispose of dead bodies as quickly as possible. So we are cremated."

Mehr, eighty, is a tall, erect, slow-moving man, careful and correct in his manners. His dark-haired, middle-aged, attractive wife served us tea and a delicious almond sweet that had just arrived in the mail from Iran, but I never learned her name. He has a trimmed white mustache and gray hair. He was a professor of law at Teheran University before the revolution of the ayatollahs and served as a deputy finance minister under the shah's government. After the shah was overthrown, Mehr brought his family to Boston. They live in a prosperous suburb in a lovely two-story stone house with a trimmed lawn. He has retired from his position as a professor of international relations at Boston University, and is the author of a number of books and articles about his religion.

"God has given man the right to choose between good and bad. Zarathustra says there are two ways to live, the good and bad ways, and the wise man chooses the good way, the path of truth. Each act has its own consequence. Zarathustra says there is no death. What happens is simply a change from one kind of life to another. Heaven is the zone of light, wisdom and happiness, says Zarathustra. When I die, I go to this zone. It is a state of consciousness. Some say there is a resurrection of the body and that heaven is a place. The terms like 'heaven' and 'resurrection' exist, but their interpretation varies."

They vary, according to Mehr, in a chronological fashion. The earliest part of the Avesta, the Gathas, do not mention a physical resurrection, although the notion of a judgment has always been present. Only later, in the writings known as the Younger Avesta, compiled around 200 CE, were heaven and hell depicted as places that exist on a physical plane. This concept continued to grow more refined as Judaism, Christianity, and Islam appeared in the world, cross-pollinating their theologies with Zoroastrianism.

Yet another great pre-Hebrew religion was operative in the Middle East along with those of the Egyptians and the Persians, and it was that of Mesopotamia and the Babylonians, the people who lived in the area known as Iraq and Syria today. A substantial written record exists from those cultures, dating back to before 2000 BCE. Babylonians also believed that life continued after death, although unlike Zoroastrians, their belief was not in a hopeful theology, but rather a worldview that life is short and full of nasty surprises. Nor does anything much better lie ahead, but perhaps it will be better than this. Davies, in his book *Death, Burial and Rebirth in the Religions of Antiquity*, cites a Babylonian poem called "Poem of the Righteous Sufferer," thought to date from 1500 BCE:

> **Who knows the will of the gods in heaven?**
> **Who understands the plans of the underworld gods?**
> **Where have mortals learnt the way of a god?**
> **He who was alive yesterday is dead today.**
> **One moment people are singing in exaltation,**
> **Another they groan like professional mourners.**

The grave was the point of passage to the underworld; it was where the journey to an eternal realm began. This is why, writes Davies, the dead were always buried, never left unburied or cremated. Burial allowed them to begin to escape from life under the sway of the upper earth's gods. Sheol, the underworld, was the fate of all mortals, but the neighborhood they would occupy once they arrived depended on how they had lived while on earth and whether their families regularly performed the ritual offerings and cared for the dead. For most, the underworld may have been a far better place to live than on earth, where death's threat was always present and life was often a struggle to satisfy hunger and thirst. In Sheol, a sufficiency of food and drink kept the deceased alive forever, although their subsistence depended to some extent on the ritual care provided by those living whom they left behind. Only those who had not been buried after death or who had lived particularly reprehensible lives would suffer eternal punishment out at the furthest reaches of Sheol.

Among the literature that survives from the great Mesopotamian culture is Gilgamesh, an epic poem built around a grand king's discovery of what it truly means to accept death and live as a mortal being. The tale of Gilgamesh is transformed by both the life and death of his closest friend, Enkidu. The king's lamentations, in Stephanie Dalley's translation, equal our own when a loved one dies: "My friend whom I love has turned to clay: Enkidu my friend whom I love has turned to clay. Am I not like him? Must I lie down too, never to rise, ever again?"

In this world, at least. Never again to stride across the ground. However, in Mesopotamian myths it is clear that life goes on below the earth under the dominion of the goddess Ereshkigal. In a text originally written in Sumerian, making it one of the oldest surviving written texts in the world, a tale is told of the journey of Ishtar from this world to the underworld. Precisely what awaits the average Sumerian or Mesopotamian in the underworld is never exactly spelled out in these myths, but it is evident that all souls are expected to have some form of body.

❧

"We will have perfect bodies in heaven," said Roberta Cross, "if we have bodies at all. I believe that after death we're united with ourselves as we were meant to be."

She is a red-haired, fair-skinned Canadian from Saskatoon, Saskatchewan, thirty-five living alone, with a quick, inquiring mind, who joined the diplomatic service in 1993 and served from 2000 to 2004 as the Canadian consul in Barcelona. When she was what she describes as "a teenager from a troubled home," she attended a Christian summer camp and became a born-again believer at the age of fifteen.

"It was then I first believed we'd have a place in heaven. And while I have let go of the other things they taught me, I still believe in that heaven. There's a lot of pain and suffering in this world, but in heaven the suffering that we have in our hearts is over, and we are united with our bodies," she told me over a *café con leche* in Barcelona one autumn morning.

"We're with our loved ones, and everyone is well. It's very peaceful. I do believe that is coming. I have bought the idea that our pain will be over and we'll enjoy eternity without suffering. To live well, I believe a person needs some kind of faith. Without it, I couldn't get through a day. Not a single day."

This civil servant with a global intelligence is a world away from James Reeves, a sixty-three-year-old black man who lives in the same small Tennessee town where he grew up and where he has owned a small barbecue restaurant for thirty-five years. Despite the distance between their lives, he echoed her: "Without my faith in heaven there's no way I could get through the day. Trying to live my faith is the only way I know how to live. I don't always make it, but I'm trying. I'd be lost without my faith."

The sign in front of his place of business reads: James BBQ. It is a low, concrete building set back from a busy highway just outside the town of Lebanon, Tennessee, and from eight to five the wooden front door is always a quarter ajar. When a customer pushes it open and steps into the dim light inside, it looks like the place was put up just last week and that next week it might be gone. That is how it has looked for the past thirty-five years. The furnishings are sparse, but solid: Formica-topped tables and ladder-back wooden chairs. The place has the feel of a bunker; not much light gets in, but there are a lot of people around Lebanon who appreciate good barbecue, and business is brisk. If a customer waiting in line to place an order notices the pictures on the walls, the impression of impermanence begins to transform. Some of them are obviously old family portraits, including daguerreotype-style sittings of well-dressed, stiff-backed black people. It appears this place has a history. A meat-and-three is offered at lunchtime, and a steady stream of people enter the shadows from the bright light outside, white and black people, men in ties and men in overalls, grandmothers and groups of young women, all kinds of people dressed in all kinds of ways.

The BBQ sandwich is a fine one with a tasty sauce, the sweet potato pie has a just-right texture in a feather-light crust, and James Reeves is about as stable and set down in this place as anybody is anywhere in the world. He is a thoughtful man of average height with a short white beard and mustache. He wears his white apron tied under his substantial belly, works up a profuse sweat over his grill each day, smiles frequently, and has a good word for everyone who comes in. The portraits on the walls include seven generations of his family, all of whom worked the land here in Wilson County, the earliest generation as slaves and later as free farmers. His is the first generation living in a time when it is impossible to make any kind of a living farming, so he learned to cook and cut hair, then opened a barbecue place with a barber shop next door. The barbering fell by the wayside, but his barbecue gained a following. He still keeps some pigs and goats and a garden on his property so he will not feel as if he has entirely quit farming, but none of his six children have any interest in agriculture or restaurants, because they have steady jobs with pension plans and health insurance. His ancestors have their final resting place in a tiny cemetery on a hill behind his land, where James likes to go and sit with his grandson on a Sunday afternoon. The congregation in which he, his son, and his grandson worship, the Dickson Chapel Missionary Baptist Church, is 130 years old. Currently about fifteen people, all of them close kin to James, show up for services on a Sunday.

One afternoon, when the lunch-hour rush was well and

truly done for the day, and he could hang up his cook's apron and come sit in a booth with me for a while, we talked about what happens after death. I expected James, because he is a rock-solid Baptist and a Bible believer, to firmly endorse physical resurrection, but I was wrong. He endorsed it, but not without reservation. "When we die, we go back to the dust, to how man was created. Then there'll be a judgment and if we haven't lived life as we should, we're going to hell. If we have, we go to heaven. Do we go in our bodies? Hmm . . . I don't think so. I think we go in the spirit, because our physical body is going back to dust. Or, maybe not. I really don't know. It would be good if we do go in our physical bodies. I would like to be able to look over there and recognize everyone. To greet them."

Lunch hour may have ended, but hungry people would continue to drift in until James closed his restaurant for the evening and went home to his piece of land out in the country, slopped his pigs, stopped off at his mother's house to say hello and check that the eighty-one-year-old woman was doing all right, and finally got back to his own house at the end of a long day. As we were sitting and talking, the door opened, and a tall, younger man stepped in out of the light.

"Ah," said James, "there's the right man to ask."

After the newcomer had placed his order with the young woman working behind the counter, James called him over to the booth and introduced him to me as the Reverend Charles Bailey, an associate pastor at another local Missionary

Baptist church. He was a big man with white paint on his dark hands. He told us he has been painting the church. He was wearing denim overalls and a paint-splattered, faded, gray baseball cap and does not miss a beat when James asked him, before he had hardly sat down, whether we have our physical bodies for eternity.

"Yes, indeed," he replied. "The Bible says we'll all be in heaven together, we'll know everybody there. So by that you can tell we're going to be in the body. Fathers, sons, mothers, daughters, we'll all join up back together. We know we're going to see each other again.

"I got to get back up to the church and keep painting. Where's Raymond at?" he asked James, rising to go get his sandwich and head out the door. "He ain't been through here? If you see him tell him I'm up to the church."

Charles Bailey bid us farewell, appearing not the least surprised or discomfited to have come in for a chopped pork sandwich and been requested to give his opinion on whether bodies are resurrected after death. Nashville is the buckle on the Bible Belt, said to have the most churches per capita of any place in the United States. In both the black and the white communities, God is often the subject of any day's conversation, the assurance of immortality a favorite topic to consider with friends and neighbors. Endless variations on the Protestant theme are all over the place, ranging from storefront churches representing the oddest of splinter groups, to huge suburban mega-churches with thousands of members, massive sanctuaries, gymnasiums, libraries, and schools all on the premises. It is not at all unusual to over-hear a hermeneutic discussion of biblical chapter and verse between two strangers while standing in line at a bank or a supermarket checkout. The Lord and religion are as present in daily life in Nashville as they are for any Muslim inter-rupting quotidian routine five times a day for prayer. Dis-cussing the nature of God's will, talking about eternal life, interpreting the Bible—these things are not restricted to polite Sunday morning gatherings in Nashville but are as much a part of daily human exchange as conversations about weather or food.

This makes for some exasperatingly boring discussions about how many angels can dance on the head of a pin, but it also makes for some great gospel music. Nothing comes closer to calling up the next world than gospel music, a giving over to the spirit, the vocal creation of a place where death is vanquished and the spirit triumphs, a place where we will see our loved ones again and be with them always. By singing this kind of music, or just listening to it, a person can blend with an ineffable sensation and be lifted in the arms of the great mystery. Both black and white Nashvillians excel at making this happen.

It has become harder over the years to believe in a heaven where we are resurrected to spend a physical eter-nity in the bodies we had on earth, praising and celebrating the Lord, or to believe in a hell where we suffer endlessly in those self-same bodies. While the great bluegrass singer Ralph Stanley or the members of the Fairfield Four, an exceptional Nashville-based gospel quartet, may believe in that biblical heaven and hell, the younger generation of Nashville voices like Emmylou Harris or Odessa Settles do not. They are the daughters of literal-minded Christian families, but they are unable to apply the old rules to their lives, unable to make them fit. The world seems more complicated, harder to decipher, than it did when their forebears were young. Yet the music still does for them what it did for their parents' generation; it is still capable of touching them in a sacred fashion, and they can make it happen for those who are listening to them sing. They pass it on. It passes through them.

"I don't believe in anything beyond this world," Emmylou Harris told me over a cup of coffee at a Nashville supermarket. "I think we have to look for heaven in this life, find it here, try to make it here, make the world a better place. Still, there's got to be some spirit. We're connected to something else."

I was not surprised to hear her say so. Anyone who has listened to her clean, pure tones of yearning and faith when she sings the classic bluegrass gospel song by Ralph Stanley, "Angel Band," or the haunting "Orphan Girl," in which her voice encompasses loss, sorrow, and hope of eternal life, knows the depth of faith she can invoke. "It's not just me making the music. I'm just a vessel for something I tap into. It's a very mystical experience. I do think there's a deep side to religion that I didn't explore in my life because for me music filled that space."

Her long, gray hair is swept up in back, and she has thin, pale, elegant hands. At fifty-eight, she is grateful for the chance to have sung to so many people over the course of a forty-year career, and she spends a good part of her time giving back to them. She is one of a handful of recording artists her age who can always be counted on to aid a decent cause, even if it is controversial. She has traveled the world singing out against nuclear power, land mines, and the death penalty. The power of music has never ceased to amaze her. "I've been spoiled with the intensity of the singing. Nothing else can compare with it."

Odessa Settles, another Nashvillian who is a lifelong singer, nods her head in agreement with this idea when I bring it up. Sacred music speaks to both the body and soul, she says, and she has spent a lifetime watching it happen. "The music touches something inside of people, it really does have the power to soothe the savage beast, like they say."

"We all have the same kinds of feelings—sorrow, love, pain. Music addresses that, not just spirituals, but all kinds of music can do that. But, for some reason, spirituals touch your soul, regardless of what kind of belief system that you have. It's soothing to the ear, it's soothing to the heart, it's soothing to the soul," she laughs.

Odessa sings spirituals, by which she means the great traditional songs of the African diaspora, the songs sung by slaves and poor free African-Americans to evoke a better world waiting. She is the fifty-two-year-old daughter of Walter Settles, who sang lead and tenor with the Fairfield

Four, one of Nashville's great gospel quartets, until his death in 1999. People were singing in her house for as long as she can remember. While her father put his musical talent at the service of gospel music, Odessa has reached farther back in the African-American tradition to the slave songs. "Gospel music is different from spirituals. Gospel music is still living, changing, but spirituals have become concretized."

Odessa believes that it is only a "soul" that goes on after death and that once we die we leave our bodies behind, she told me. That is not what she was raised to believe. She was raised in a Bible-ordered world. "We grew up in the Christian way of thinking. We actually did believe that we would see our loved ones on the other side. We grew up thinking that, but I don't believe it anymore."

Annie Robinson does. At eighty-four she is still going out a couple of days a week to clean houses for white people who, after decades, have become more like her family than her employers. She helps keep their lives in order. She is a short woman with a round, crocheted cap of colors on her head. She moves slowly but steadily through her day's work, doing laundry, vacuuming carpets. She has been going to the same Missionary Baptist church in Nashville for thirty-five years. "I would like to think we all go to heaven, but that would make it too easy on the Devil. I believe in heaven and hell. You have to take your punishment somewhere. You get what you deserve. Now, it's true some people are so good, even though they are not Christians, I've seen some so good that you can't hardly think they'd go to hell.

I think when you go to heaven you get your body back healed and whole.

"My family always laughs at me because if something gets too heavy on me I always look forward to some help from my mother. She has been gone a long time. I get a lot of laughs from my family when I say my mother would do this or that. But, I feel like my mother is present when I need her. It may sound funny to some, but that's just how I feel."

Hell still burns brightly for some believers, but for many it has lost its glow. In 1997, a Gallup poll reported that while 72 percent of people in the United States believed in a heaven, only 56 percent professed to believe in hell. Of course, that means over half the people in the U.S. still believed in eternal damnation for the unsaved. Over the centuries since they were founded, all three major monotheisms have posited both a heaven and a hell, enjoyed or suffered in the resurrected body. The idea that we shall be resurrected from the dead to spend eternity in a body is a cornerstone belief of Christianity and Islam, and consistently recurs in Judaism.

It is hard to imagine that the young man's body on the table in Charles Harlan's workplace is going to do duty ever again. The scalp has been rolled back down and sewn on the head in the back where it won't show in an open casket, the flaps of flesh pulled together over the chest cavity and laced closed with a wicked, long, curved, silver needle and white thread as thick as twine. Without the organs beneath, the sewn flesh of his chest and stomach is collapsed in on itself like a leaky football, but the sunken chest and in-fallen belly will not be noticeable after the funeral home dresses the body in its burial clothes.

"This boy could have been alive today if he'd gone to the doctor," says Harlan, peeling off his thin, white, latex gloves and washing his hands. "He was definitely in respiratory distress for a day or two, but he probably thought it was allergies or asthma and would get better.

"You see those lungs?" he gestures toward the bucket of organs. "That's what killed him. There's almost no air in them, they're very congested. He needed to be hospitalized, but he didn't make it."

The next day, Harlan is scheduled to do an autopsy on an exhumed body, already nine months in the grave. He invites me to come and watch. "They're the worst," he wrinkles his nose. "Any flesh left on them just falls away. And the smell . . . ," he shakes his head. I politely decline.

For all the decaying flesh he has seen, Charles Harlan is a Southern Baptist who sings in the choir, served for years as a deacon in his church, and firmly believes that after death he will be resurrected to spend a heavenly eternity in his body. "If God can create the earth, He can do anything. Why try to put limitations on what God can do? He can put our organs back. He can cause the body to exist again. Maybe we don't need our bodies in heaven, but if God wants us to have them, He can give them back to us. And I believe He will."

Details of *The Garden of Earthly Delights* by Hieronymous Bosch. *Courtesy of Museo Nacional del Prado.*

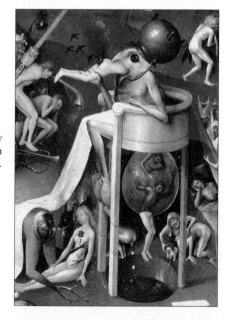

Detail of *The Triumph of Death* by Bruegel the Elder. It hangs across Room 54-A in the Prado across from the Bosch. *Courtesy of Museo Nacional del Prado.*

The War against Death

Talking to a peasant one day, I suggested to him the hypothesis that there might indeed be a God who governs heaven and earth, a Consciousness or Conscience of the Universe, but that even so it would not be sufficient reason to assume that the soul of every man was immortal in the traditional and concrete sense. And he replied: "Then, what good is God?"

From *The Tragic Sense of Life in Men and Nations*
by Miguel de Unamuno

Each of those 100 billion people who have lived and died since the last Ice Age were different from one another. Each had his or her own unique set of chromosomes, a once-in-eternity DNA. If, somehow, that exact genetic combination could be recreated, reconstructed, then we could all live again in the body that was only ever ours in the whole entire history of the universe. Of course, that does not mean we would be the same person, since our experiences and environment would be different and we would not have our old memories. However, if we were capable of recreating our bodies and could keep our brains preserved in some sort of suspended animation ready for that moment when our flesh lived again, perhaps we could be resurrected to another life perhaps we could live forever.

"Death is an imposition on the human race, and no longer acceptable. Man has all but lost his ability to accommodate himself to personal extinction; he must now proceed physically to overcome it. In short, to kill death: to put an end to his own mortality as a certain consequence of being born."

That is how Alan Harrington begins his book *The Immortalist*, his call-to-arms for the human race to unite against death. The great, uplifting, transformative quest of our species, he asserts, is our rebellion against and resistance to the inevitability of death. Soon, wrote Harrington in 1969, science will make it possible to live forever. The surrender of this body to old age and death will no longer be necessary. Ours are the last generations that will have to struggle and die. No higher, more noble calling exists for humans than to advance the race minutely ever forward toward that day when people are not born to die but are free to live forever and construct a "utopia beyond time" here on earth.

Harrington was an elegantly dressed, well-spoken, New York City writer who consorted with the likes of Jack Kerouac and Timothy Leary. He wrote with a clear eye for the foibles of his time and an expansive imagination about what we could and must do in the future to free the human race from death. Alas, if such a liberation comes, it will be too late for him, as it will likely be for all of us. Alan Harrington died in 1997, at the age of seventy-nine, in his bed. Despite a lifetime of railing against death's dominion, he accepted it with dignity and tranquility during his last hours, according to Internet reports from those who were there.

In addition to writing a powerful antideath manifesto addressed to the human race, he used his book to explore various hopeful signs of progress during the late 1960s in the struggle to achieve life everlasting. One was cryonics, the process of freezing a body immediately following death and maintaining it frozen at 128 degrees below zero—for centuries if necessary—until such time as the technology will exist to thaw it, bring it back to life, and successfully treat the cause of death.

The father of this pseudoscience was a physics professor in Detroit, Robert Ettinger, who began by writing fiction about the possibility of freezing and reviving the dead, and became convinced, the more he thought about and investigated the idea, that it was not science fiction but science fact. In 1962, he wrote a book called *The Prospect of Immortality*.

From the start, it enjoyed decent sales. No surprise, as by the end of the book's first paragraph Ettinger is assuring his readers, "Most of us now living have a chance for personal, physical immortality."

The Cryonics Society of Michigan was formed in 1967 with Ettinger as its president, and it later became the Cryonics Institute. In 1972, Alcor, the other major player in the cryonics business, was incorporated in California and eventually relocated to Scottsdale, Arizona. In 2005, both companies were still in business. A third cryonics company, the Cryonics Society of California, founded in the late 1960s, went out of business within a few years, and at least nine preserved bodies were reported to have thawed out and decomposed after the firm went under.

Up until 2001, both the Cryonics Institute and Alcor used essentially the same process to preserve dead human beings. It is succinctly described on the institute's Web site: "Cryonics doesn't consist simply of 'freezing' people, but of preparing them in a way so to minimize freezing damage as such. . . . To that end a patient is prepared with anticoagulant, cooled as rapidly as possible, and is taken to facilities where a full perfusion can be performed (perfusion being the process of removing the patient's blood and replacing it with a cryoprotectant solution which keeps the body from being excessively damaged during the course of freezing). Then the patient is gradually cooled in dry ice, and finally placed in a liquid nitrogen immersion at a temperature [around $-130°C$] at which further deterioration is negligible."

The first human was frozen in 1967, a seventy-three-year-old Southern California retired psychology professor named James Bedford. By 2004, the Cryonics Institute's membership stood at 450, with fifty bodies in cryopreservation at the Michigan facility. Alcor reported that it had more than 650 members, with fifty-nine people in cryopreservation. In the case of Alcor, some of those were not entire bodies but only heads.

With neuropreservation, as Alcor calls it, the head is severed from the body with major aortas intact and undergoes a process called vitrification, which uses a special fluid chemically engineered to solidify at extremely low temperatures and which maintains tissue intact in a "glassy" or vitrified condition, causing almost no tissue damage. The severed head is stored in a special container at -190°C. Neurosuspension, as practiced at Alcor, is an alternative procedure for those who believe that bodies will be easy to create and that the important thing is to preserve their brains so that, implanted in a body, they can resume life where they left off, with their original memories and learned lessons intact.

Until recently, both the Cryonics Institute and Alcor offered essentially the same services, keeping a body in cold storage and guaranteeing to continue doing so for centuries if need be. Then, in 2001, Alcor began practicing vitrification and neuropreservation. The Cryonics Institute still was not offering the head-only option at its Michigan facility in 2005. The decision, the institute explained on its Web site, was made on both scientific and public relations grounds. The science to restore a brain to life does not exist yet, and the brains must be maintained until such time as it does. Furthermore, the institute's Web site pointed out without even a hint of humor, neurosuspension is a public relations nightmare. It is one thing to tell grieving survivors that their loved ones are going to have their bodies frozen so they will not rot, but quite another to say you are going to sever their heads and keep them in suspended animation for centuries.

Cryonics is not pure snake oil. The science of cryobiology is real and growing. What happens to living matter at low temperatures is of interest to people in a number of fields, and experiments have shown that animal subjects can be frozen for many hours and revived with little damage. Human sperm, as well, can thrive after periods of frozen inactivity. Many of the theories expounded by cryonics proponents have a sprinkling of verifiable science in them. The recent development of a field called *nanotechnogy*, using supremely tiny microinstruments to manipulate matter on an atomic level, has been embraced by cryonics promoters as the way in which damage to brains or bodies will be repaired at that future moment when they are thawed to live again.

What is more dubious is that any of the frozen bodies or brains currently stored in cryonics facilities will see that moment. Extended freezing and subsequent warming can put their own fatal stress on cells and tissues. Cures for many of the diseases that killed these people are still far away, as is the ability to thaw the tissue without doing any harm to it. The facilities will have to stay intact and functioning a long time to reach the era in which these dead bodies can be revivified and cured.

Reading the online arguments of neurosuspension versus whole-body preservation is a bizarre experience. It is disorienting, implying a whole different way of looking at the world, our lives, and what possibilities exist for outwitting death. That is, for those who can afford it. Because whether a person opts for putting only a head in cold storage or keeping body and brain preserved, it will not come cheaply. The minimum for neuropreservation using vitrification technology at Alcor was $80,000 in 2005 and for a whole-body suspension at the Cryonics Institute, done by preservation in liquid nitrogen, an outlay of $28,000 was required.

Harrington points out in *The Immortalist* that at the prices charged by cryonics companies only rich people will enjoy resurrection, and he raises the possibility that, should the process ever prove successful, the poor will not stand for it. In the end, he dismisses the potential of cryonics as a long-term weapon in the war against death. Its direct confrontation with the grim reaper and defiant assertion that death can be cheated endeared cryonics to him, although Harrington was too astute an observer to place his hopes for liberation from the grave in something so problematic. For the winning weapon in the war against death he looked to James Watson and Francis Crick and the science of genetics that they illuminated. Harrington wrote as early as 1969 that the great hope for human immortality lay coiled within our chromosomes. The life-stuff of DNA would serve as the ultimate weapon against death, and he believed that within its spirals lay the answer to prolonging ourselves indefinitely. It is to science that humans must look to carry the battle against death forward.

"Humanity's radical wing, growing stronger by the decade, has devoted its energies for more than five hundred years not to joining the company of imagined gods but rather to overthrowing the celestial ruling class, replacing these deities and even finally becoming them," he wrote. "The slow-working universal solvent developed to accomplish this end has been inductive research.

"Probings into every corner of knowledge carry forward the race's enduring project: to gain complete dominance (divine power) over all processes that might affect the human form. . . . Camouflaged by outward humility, what we call pure science serves as the arm of pure rebellion. It aspires to nothing less than supreme being. In theory, the race's radical wing moves ahead disinterestedly searching, but in the end—beyond the succession of limited objectives along the way—the quarry being hunted down is death."

Humans are not likely to do away with death any time soon. Right now and for the foreseeable future, genetic engineering advances will not help people so much to live forever as to live better longer and suffer less while they are alive. A hundred years ago, a white male's life expectancy was around fifty, and infectious diseases played havoc with people while they lived, carrying away many at an early age. Now diseases like polio and yellow fever are not a threat to most *Homo sapiens*. Instead, this generation is living long enough to suffer things like Parkinson's and Alzheimer's in great numbers. Cancer thins the ranks of those whom these other diseases miss; diabetes brings still others to the grave. All of these may possibly be mitigated or eliminated by treating them at a genetic level.

Despite the multitude of potentially fatal diseases and accidents that abound in our everyday world, people in the developed world *do* live longer than they used to, and any advance that extends, even by a short time, the average life expectancy is one more step along what has already been a long road. In the time of the Greeks and Romans, according to Gerald Gruman in *A History of Ideas about the Prolongation of Life*, a male's life expectancy did not go far beyond twenty. A millennium passed, but a man's allotted number of years increased at a crawl. By the start of the 1700s, it was only up to around thirty, but by the beginning of the 1900s, a white male could expect to live fifty years, by 1950 that was up to sixty-six, and it reached seventy-five in 2001, according to U.S. Census Bureau figures.

In the 1950s and '60s, gerontology was a lackluster field of medicine and research, mostly having to do with treating the ravages of old age, but as the population has grown older, the focus has shifted to postponing, if not entirely preventing, those ravages. Gerontology has become increasingly visible in the media, in popular culture, and in the market-place. Not a week goes by without a new press release about one or another antiaging discovery.

People willing to pay large sums of money for an outside chance at living longer are not in short supply at the beginning of the twenty-first century. They will gladly put down their money for the remote possibility of even a few extra years. When this is not on offer, they are still happy to part with a small fortune on treatments and products designed to erase, prevent, or disguise the visible physical signs of aging—drooping muscles, wrinkles, and paunches

In the long run, it does not matter. Sooner or later the muscles weaken, the body grows frail, serious decline begins, and life ends in death. In the short run, however, a lot is at stake for individuals, and since at least as far back in recorded history as the Greek alchemists, people have dedicated their lives to searching for the key to how the whole thing works—the physical formula to extend life indefinitely. The Greeks reasoned that all materials are forms of one basic element and that if that element could be created at will, physical immortality would be possible—the creation of life everlasting through alchemy. The concept is echoed in the excitement with which stem cells are viewed today as the building blocks for new organs and tissues and nerves. The genetic code is the equivalent of the alchemist's "philosopher's stone," which would turn base metals into gold, mortal flesh into life everlasting.

Alchemy was practiced around the world, from China to

Arabia to Europe, and the investigation into the properties of life's basic elements yielded copious useful information. The elements, the basic materials of life both healthy and toxic, all had their analogues in the human spirit, according to the alchemists, and were refined and transmuted both in the actual physical element and in the inner world present in every human being. The search for transmutation lasted until the mid-1600s, when it was itself transmuted into chemistry. In 1661, Robert Boyle broke with the Aristotelian idea of mutable elements and proposed that elements are irreducible. His work is often cited as the moment when science as we know it today edged alchemy out of the laboratory door, even though Boyle himself continued to conduct alchemical experiments all his life.

Inductive science took over the search for what people are made of and, in the struggle against senescence, that process by which human machinery ages and wears out. Today, scientific investigation is firmly in control our hopes and longings for immortality are carried forward under its standard, propelled by slow, expensive work in laboratories. Sometimes it produces nanotechnology and organ transplants and at other times, things for more mundane uses, from breast implants to collagen therapy or treatments for erectile dysfunction.

Viagra, for instance, is only the latest, and perhaps the most effective of a long line of modern-day substances employed to help with impotence in aging European men. Osborn Segerberg, Jr., reviews them in his book *The Immortality Factor*. He begins with the method developed

by one of the founders of the medical science of
endocrinology, the eminent French-Irish physician
Charles-Édouard Brown-Séquard, born in 1817. Segerberg
recounts that when Brown-Séquard was an old man, he took
a young wife, his third, but as his body weakened, he was
unable to enjoy her delights. In front of the Société de
Biologie in Paris on June 1, 1889, he told the assembled
biologists of how only two and a half weeks earlier he had
made a purée of a young dog's testicle, filtered the juice
from the mash, and injected it into his leg.

The change, he told the meeting, was astonishing. He
had recovered his strength, felt as if he was thirty years
younger, and told the biologists, "Today I was able 'to pay
a visit' to my young wife." His lecture was virtually the end
of his career, as his colleagues derided him mercilessly. His
young wife eventually left him, and Segerberg tells us he
died five years after his lecture of a stroke.

This is one among thousands of tales, found all around
the globe and in every age, of those who have endeavored
by hook or crook to stay young. It never works forever, but
it does not have to. Whether it is Bulgarian yogurt, or pow-
dered mummy, or crushed bull's testicles, or vitamin treatments, if it just helps hold off senescence for a bit, it is
worth its weight in gold. Of course, the best method for
achieving longevity may be to live moderately and sensibly
and avoid excess and stress—exactly the same recommenda-
tion made by Hippocrates to the Greeks: abstinence from all
things that shorten life and moderation in all the rest.

Even those people who avoid diseases and health problems all their lives are going to die. Death is somehow programmed into cells, perhaps into every cell. Laboratories all over the world are working on the question of programmed cell death and whether it can be genetically controlled. Science is seeking the switches that turn on the program and the means to affect either the program or the switch. Whoever makes off with that patent will have the beginnings of a substantial fortune.

Ben Bova asks in his book *Immortality:* "Is there a death gene?

"Deep within the cells of our bodies, is there a triggering mechanism that tells the cell when it is time to die? Is aging—senescence—truly inevitable?

"Is there a built-in clock in each of our cells that sooner or later starts the process of aging and programmed cell death? If there is, can we prevent it from causing death? Can we . . . learn how to reset the clock of senescence?

"If we an understand how our genes work and map out which genes perform which functions in human cells, we may be able not only to correct genetic disorders but also to discover if death genes exist—and how to cancel their action."

Scientists grow ever closer to understanding the mechanisms by which we age, and some predict that soon people will be able to retard or entirely switch off those mechanisms at a cellular level. Advances in the struggle against aging may be coming at a faster rate, but a long road remains ahead. Leonard Hayflick, a revered name among gerontological researchers, has pointed out that even if cures were found for Alzheimer's, stroke, diabetes, Parkinson's disease, cancer, and hepatitis, only about fifteen years would be added to our average life expectancy.

In 1961, Hayflick announced his discovery that cells have a finite limit on the number of times they will reproduce. Today, the Hayflick limit, as it is named, is part of the foundation of antiaging research. Cells that cease to reproduce are eventually dead cells. A lot of people are spending a lot of time researching why cells stop producing healthy replicas of themselves when they reach the Hayflick limit. One theory is that the mechanism that cuts off normal cell reproduction is located at the ends of chromosomes, in the telomeres. These are shortened every time cells reproduce and at a certain point they are so short that the cell cannot reproduce. A lot of research has focused on these ends of the chromosomes. The hope is that if telomeres can stay healthy and functioning, the body will not age. In his book *Merchants of Immortality*, Stephen Hall writes that telomere research reintroduced the term *immortality* to serious scientific discourse.

Despite all the research underway, Hayflick himself has predicted that the average life expectancy in the developed world will not reach ninety by the end of the twenty-first century. In a June 2002 *Scientific American* paper, "No Truth to the Fountain of Youth," Hayflick and two other leading aging researchers, Jay Olshansky and Bruce Carnes, pointed out that over the twentieth century, most of the advances in life expectancy of an individual at birth occurred because of "dramatic declines in mortality risks in childhood and early adult life."

New ground in the struggle to extend life expectancy will be harder to win. "In fact, even eliminating all aging-related causes of death currently written on the death certificates of the elderly will not increase human life expectancy by more than fifteen years," wrote Hayflick and his colleagues. "To exceed this limit, the underlying processes of aging that increase vulnerability to all the common causes of death will have to be modified."

Not everyone is so conservative in their predictions. Hall's book reports that since the early 1800s, the optimum life span has been increasing by about three months a year, and some scientists believe the trend will continue indefinitely. Most optimists at this moment put their hope in one of two developing new medical fields: nanotechnology and the use of stem cells and genetic engineering. In theory, nanotechnology could eventually shape atoms into any desired form, including a human being, a new heart, food, housing, or anything else. It has, say its proponents, the potential to end the eons when people had to live by the sweat of their brows. We could have all we need on earth and all we need to live on indefinitely.

Genetic engineering could provide healthy new organs as replacements for those gone bad, could replace a bad chromosome with a good one, and could also open the possibility of actually cloning one's individual self and repeating it end-lessly. All of this is made possible by genetic science and stem cell research advances. Stem cells contain the basic construction code for the entire body, and with them it may be possible to grow healthy, compatible organs and tissues or to replace a bad genetic code with a better one. Because the best possibility is to work with stem cells harvested from embryonic tissues, the entire field is surrounded by political and ethical considerations, but this is not likely to delay the use of stem cells for long. If it fulfills its early promise, the technology to develop compatible organs and tissues on demand would radically change many peoples' lives as well as represent a huge investment opportunity.

We now recognize that the uniqueness of our individual genome means that each of us is, in theory, immortal and resurrectable. Once the technology is at hand with which to reproduce my own genetic code, the possibility exists for my living again no matter how long since I died. Or perhaps people will store genetic samples of themselves to be reconstructed when a cure exists for whatever killed them. These things are no longer the stuff of science fiction. Given even the smallest part of our former selves, we could theoretically be cloned—we could live again. Of course, it is only the body that would be recreated, without mind, memory, emotions, experiential data, or any other components of our mental being. But perhaps eventually the possibility will exist of transferring the mind to some sort of hard disk and holding it in reserve to transfer back to the resurrected body.

Suddenly, even the idea of neurosuspension—of freezing our heads for use at a later date—does not seem entirely preposterous.

The idea that each of us is part of a record was illustrated by Jews in their concept of the "Book of Life" two thousand years ago, the book in which is written the names of all the righteous who have ever lived. While only a handful of Old Testament references point to such a record, the idea was incorporated into the liturgy of Rosh Hashanah and Yom Kippur worship services, the two highest holy days. During services for both holidays, congregants offer a prayer asking God to remember and write their names in the Book of Life. The image also reappears in the last pages of the New Testament, in Revelation 20:12: "And I saw the dead, small and great, stand before God; and the books were opened: and another book was opened which is the book of life: and the dead were judged out of those things which were written in the books, according to their works."

It turns out that, at least in terms of genetic composition, each of us does have our own page. Our codes all exist within the vast possibilities of the genetic code for our species, and they are written in the tiniest parts of us that we leave all over the house. A record of our complete physical bodies is present in something as insignificant as a lock of hair follicle, a fingernail, a fleck of skin left on a bone, or dried saliva on a cigarette butt. From any of these, our precise and individual DNA can be read.

Orthodox Jews believe that one bone, the Luz, is enough

to serve as the seed to generate a whole resurrected and eternal body when the Messiah finally comes. "The seed disintegrates and gives birth to the new plant, and so, too, the old body decomposes, but the new one springs forth from its dust," wrote Robert Goldenberg in an essay for *Death and Afterlife*. "This conception led to the idea that even as the body returns to dust, a small bone in the base of the spine, a bone called Luz, never entirely disappears; this bone eventually becomes the kernel around which the rest of the resurrected body can take form."

In his book *Reincarnation and Judaism: The Journey of the Soul*, DovBer Pinson writes about the traditional current of Jewish thought that believed in reincarnation. That such a belief even existed comes as a surprise to most Jews, but Pinson uncovers strong beliefs in reincarnation in Judaism, most often in the kabbalistic tradition. He traces reincarnation all the way back to the truths revealed, "both mundane and mystical," to Moses on Mount Sinai. Ample writings of learned rabbis from the Middle Ages attest to the part reincarnation played in medieval Jewish thought about the afterlife.

In his book, Pinson emphasizes that reincarnation is a consolation prize, second-best, and something less than truly living forever. It is not the resurrection of the dead but merely a stopgap transition for the soul until that singular historical moment arrives and history ends, when we rise up to live forever. "True immortality is attained only through the eternity of the actual physical body," he writes:

"This is the concept of resurrection of the dead. The *Midrash* states, 'There is a small bone in the body, the Luz, which never disintegrates, and from this bone, the entire body will be resurrected.' When the prophet Isaiah speaks of the resurrection, he says, 'God will revive the dead.' He does not say that God will rebuild the body and will then create a new body, rather God will revive the body, meaning that there are still remnants of the body which have not disappeared. From this minute bone (it may be the size of an atom or even smaller), God will resurrect the entire body. Hence, this small Luz bone is the immortality of the physical body."

It is this belief that the body will rise again, sprouted from the Luz, that is at the root of orthodox Judaism's rejection of cremation.

This is the exact line in this book on which I was working the day my eighty-eight-year-old mother died. Cremation was fine, she had told us, when the time came. Although a Jew, she never cared a fig for orthodox thinking about much of anything. She cared for family, friends, books, doing the right thing. Things like that. My mother passed her last years in the small New England coastal town where my brother set down roots and grew his own family, over a thousand miles north of the Jewish cemetery in Nashville, the city where she was born and where she raised us. She wanted her ashes to rest beside the grave holding my father's remains, her husband of forty-seven years. A blank gravestone was waiting there, marking the spot.

Now the blank is filled in with dates. Her ashes are there.
My good and loving mother is gone.
Gone where? Tell me, friend.
Speak.

"We don't want to be cremated. It says in the Bible, 'You are dust and you shall return to dust,' but not cremation. Cremation no," said Zalman Posner, eighty-one, a retired Orthodox Jewish rabbi who spent fifty years as the leader of Nashville's Orthodox community, a congregation that musters one hundred people to worship on a Saturday morning. He still has a rich, strong, sonorous voice, a luxuriant salt-and-pepper beard and sidelocks, and an unshakable confidence in his own tradition, the Chabad Hassidim.

"I'm really shocked that some of the people insist on cremation. '*Ki afar atah v'el afar tashuv*,' it says in Genesis. You shall return to dust. And then, after we found out what happened in Germany, in Auschwitz . . . they burned them. They burned them alive. Burning them? This is a Nazi thing to do."

Of course, many of the people who astonish Zalman Posner by opting for cremation are reform Jews. It doesn't matter if you're cremated or buried, said Randall Falk, a retired Reform Jewish rabbi in Nashville. Smooth-shaven, nearly bald at eighty-three, he still spends half a day every weekday at Nashville's Ohabi Shalom Temple, where he led the much larger reform congregation of a few thousand for twenty-six years.

"What happens to your body after you're dead is of little consequence," he told me. "What matters is how you lived your life here. What happens after a person dies we don't know. One of the good things about Judaism is we don't try to guess. We don't have a heaven and a hell and all that nonsense, although what happens after death is very much a part of our tradition. At the end of every service we say the *kaddish*, which is our affirmation in some form of life after death. It affirms that there is some power greater than our own from whence we come and to which we return, but it's very vague."

Both Orthodox Judaism and the Jewish kabbalistic tradition have clear and certain expectations of an afterlife and a resurrection. However, a renunciation of these beliefs has become common among Reform Jews. Because they are more numerous, their views or nonviews about the afterlife have obscured the older Orthodox tradition. "Ask most Jewish adults what happens after death, and they don't have an answer, because it's not something that we emphasize," said Falk. "One of the things that has always attracted me to Judaism is that it's a religion of this life with very little speculation about what goes beyond, although we do have a belief that something does. We concentrate on this life and what our obligations are here, and what will be after death will be and will take care of itself."

The concept of an afterlife no longer seems to exist for a large number of practicing Jews, and has not for quite a while. A 1965 Gallup poll asked the question, "Do you think your soul will live on after death?" Eighty-three percent of the Catholics who responded believed so, 78 percent of the Protestants, and only 17 percent of the Jews. Forty-six percent of the Jews said no, and 37 percent said they did not know. While Christians have always agreed on salvation and resurrection as cornerstones of their faith, Jews have never reached a consensus on what happens after death. While some Jews believe the Messiah will come and we will be resurrected to eternal life, many others assert that it is the now that matters, and that we must lead righteous lives without expecting reward after death. What happens after we die is unknowable, and as mere mortals it shows a lack of respect to even waste time speculating on the subject.

At the beginning of Christian history, traditional Jewish believers fell into two main groups: the Sadducees and the Pharisees. The former were the aristocratic class, who leaned toward a Hellenistic interpretation of the Bible, and did not believe in a messiah or a resurrection. A life well lived and the continuation of the Jewish people were the important things these were what Jews should strive for, not wasting time worrying about death and its consequences. Robert Goldenberg wrote, "To drop the concepts of Heaven and Hell from Christianity is to drop the need for salvation, and that is to remove the heart from the Christian religion. To remove these concepts from Judaism leaves certain questions unanswered, but allows the basic outline of the religion to stand. . . . Classic Jewish thinking saw national catastrophe, not individual extinction, as the worst imaginable disaster; the meaning of history, not the meaning of life, has been the ultimate concern of Judaic thinking."

Classical Greek thinking also had a tremendous influence on Hebrew thinkers. It generated still another current of belief, which fed into Judaism. Plato firmly posited an afterlife, but only the individual soul would experience it; there would be no postmortem existence for the body. The soul would survive to live, bodiless, in union with God. Immortality existed, but not resurrection. The highest expression of divinity in humans here on earth was philosophy—dedicating our intellects to considering the meaning of life. In doing so, the soul would be refined during this life by philosophical reflection and would separate from the body at death to pass on to an eternal existence.

One place in which Greek philosophy stands out as a building block of Hebrew thought is in the writings of Philo of Alexandria, or Philo Judaeus, who lived from about 20 BCE to 50 CE, and was the most prolific writer among Hellenistic Jewish philosophers. He believed, according to Alan Segal's *Life After Death*, that the immortality of the soul must be gained in this life by perfecting our intellectual and moral faculties so that our souls can ascend to a realized plane forever. Philo was born into a wealthy and learned family in Alexandria, one of the most cultured, learned cities in the world at the time. His writings are concerned with reconciling Greek philosophy and the Old Testament, synthesizing Platonism and the Bible.

For Philo, the soul came from God, from the eternal ground

of being, and after death, if it had been maintained well by philosophical reflection and striving, it returned. "Ideally, the Jew should be a philosopher who like Philo led the retired life of a thinker preparing the soul for its celestial ascent," write Colleen McDannell and Bernhard Lang in *Heaven: A History*. "Preparation for death served as a basis for meditation, rather than for getting ready for a resurrected society."

The Pharisees, on the other hand, believed in an eventual resurrection and were part of a tradition that reached back to Zoroastrianism. Zarathustra's doctrine of resurrection is indisputably present in a part of early Jewish thinking. The clearest biblical example is in Ezekiel 37. On the valley plain, before the prophet's eyes, the bones of the dead rise up to form living, breathing bodies again, and in verses 12 to 14, the Lord God speaks through Ezekiel: "Behold, O my people, I will open your graves and cause you to come up out of your graves, and bring you into the land of Israel. And you shall know that I am the Lord when I have opened your graves, O my people, and brought you up out of your graves, and I shall put my spirit in you and you shall live . . . ."

The two other books in the Old Testament that promise resurrection of the dead are Isaiah and Daniel. Isaiah 26:19 promises: "Thy dead men shall live, together with my dead body shall they arise. Awake and sing, ye that dwell in dust: for thy dew is as the dew of herbs, and the earth shall cast out the dead."

Daniel, according to Alan Segal, can be dated quite precisely to 168 BCE, considerably later than Isaiah. His is a mixed promise and threat: "And many of them that sleep in the dust of the earth shall awake, some to everlasting life, and some to shame and everlasting contempt."

Flavius Josephus, the historian who lived around the beginning of the Common Era, described the Pharisees as intelligent, abstemious, and living in harmony with one another, according to Segal. They were largely made up of scribes and craftsmen. Josephus also described the Pharisees' idea of the afterlife: "Every soul, they maintain, is imperishable but the soul of the good alone passes into another body, while the souls of the wicked suffer eternal punishment."

A judgment will take place, according to Pharaisical thought, and the "good" shall be resurrected to spend eternity in the presence of God. Perhaps the most well known of the Pharisees was the Apostle Paul, whose revelation on the road to Damascus convinced him that Jesus was the Messiah and that the end-time was upon him. Paul also believed that a judgment would follow the resurrection and that the righteous would then spend eternity in the presence of God and Jesus Christ. He did not believe that our old, buried bodies would live again, but that we would be clothed in a new body, as he explained in 1 Corinthians 15:42–44: "So also is the resurrection of the dead. It is sown in corruption; it is raised in incorruption:

"It is sown in dishonor; it is raised in glory: it is sown in weakness; it is raised in power:

"It is sown a natural body; it is raised a spiritual body. There is a natural body and there is a spiritual body."

In their book *Heaven: A History*, McDannell and Lang write that Paul believed God prepares another home or garment for the soul after the death of the body. "To move from one garment into the other necessitates a perilous journey, literally a death. . . . Like Jesus, dead Christians also leave their physical bodies in the dust. God will eventually provide the dead with a new and imperishable 'spiritual' body. Paul's language does not imply the restoration of the physical human body."

As might be expected given the distance between our lives and the time in which the Apostle Paul was writing, many different interpretations of his words exist. "An immense amount has been written about how we are to understand the notion of the spiritual body, in Greek the *soma pneumatikon*," wrote religious studies professor Terence Penelhum, in 1997, about Paul's message in 1 Corinthians 15. "Those who do not wish to think that the spiritual body is a body at all lay much stress on the fact that Paul also says (verse 50) that flesh and blood can never possess the Kingdom of God. . . . But it does not follow from this that those who inherit the Kingdom will not have physical bodies, only that they will not have corruptible bodies. I think he means that the *soma pneumatikon* is not a spirit but an incorruptible body, that is, the body of a person who has been redeemed from corruption."

That incorruptible body is at the heart of the Nicene

Creed, adopted by the Church in 325 CE and incorporated into Christian liturgies all over the world. It affirms belief in the Church, baptism, forgiveness, and the resurrection of the dead and in fact concludes: "I look for the resurrection of the dead and the life to come."

Jon Roebuck is pastor of the Woodmont Baptist Church, located in one of Nashville's richer white enclaves. He is forty-five but looks quite a few years younger, with short, sandy hair and blue eyes. Born and raised in Georgia, he has spent his life in the Southeast. He has a thick southern accent and a sonorous voice and is a self-described "aviation buff" with a pilot's license, who told me his main goal in this life is to fly a Cessna Piper Cub at three thousand feet across the United States sometime before he dies. As far as what will happen after he dies, he believes he will get a new body, a more perfect body, and that what happens to the one he currently inhabits is irrelevant.

"Cremation, or decomposition, or airplane crash, anything. I believe there's a bodily resurrection after that, the one the Scriptures speak of, but they also speak of a *new* body. I tend to look at this current body as a temporary body. If God had intended us to live forever in these bodies, they would be more perfect than they are. Things like heart disease, diabetes, cancer say that these bodies, even working as well as they do, are still not perfect machines. God has something better in store for us. I do believe we'll be recognized and be able to recognize each other, that we'll have a type of physical form somehow similar to what we have now, but something about it will be more perfect, more complete."

When I spoke with him in his study at the church, he was wearing a Polo sport shirt and checked pants. His master's degree is from the Southern Baptist Theological Seminary in Louisville, Kentucky, a right-wing, conservative institution. Roebuck has pastored around the Southeast and has been at Woodmont Baptist for six years. The congregation numbers around fourteen hundred—"Enough folks to say grace over," he chuckled contentedly—and he reaches another eighty thousand people on a half-hour television broadcast by an ABC affiliate in Nashville that can be picked up off a satellite dish as far away as San Francisco or Santo Domingo.

The church is a large brick building that has been added on to time and again. The congregation's families have incomes substantially higher than the U.S. median. It is a virtually all-white group of worshipers, and on Sundays the parking lot is chock-a-block full of SUVs, Cadillacs, Mercedes Benzes, and Lincolns. The pastor says he takes the church's social responsibilities seriously, and the congregation participates in a number of the city's interdenominational efforts to aid the poor, including one called Room at the Inn, in which, twice a year, the homeless are given a night's shelter inside the church, and congregants volunteer to stay there with them, keeping watch. Rosebud tells me:

"There are obviously churches that emphasize social gospel in terms of caring for the poor and meeting those needs. I think that's an important dimension of Christian faith. We are saved to serve, and we do have an obligation, but I think our number-one focus is trying to bring people into God's kingdom through faith in Jesus Christ. That's priority one. If you're not in God's kingdom, then you don't have the hope of resurrection."

Jon Roebuck has, like so many of Nashville's Christian faithful, "some real good friends who are Jewish." He would like to be able to say he believes there is room in heaven for them, that eternal damnation is not going to be their lot, but unfortunately, he said, Scripture indicates otherwise. Those who do not accept Christ are not going to make it. "Based on the revelation that I have through God's word in the New Testament, Scripture is clear that we gain access to the Father through Christ alone. So if I am a Christian, if I have made that profession of faith in my life, then my eternal salvation is secure. If I'm not, then I'm on shaky ground.

"I'm not saying that non-Christians aren't going to gain access to heaven. That's God's call. God is judge, and as creator of all things has a right to decide who gets in and who doesn't, but in my understanding, eternal life is secured by those who are in Christ."

So what waits for the unsaved, the preterite? By Pastor Roebuck's lights, it is hell. "The joyful part about being a Christian is that according to the New Testament, Christians receive eternal life through their faith in Christ. What happens to the non-Christians, to the Jews specifically, where do they go? If you believe in the reality of heaven, then you have to believe in the reality of hell. If there's some kind of eternal existence that you live in the light of God's glory, then there's also got to be an eternal existence that is an eternal separation from God and that exists for those who have not found God through faith in Christ."

Christians did not invent the idea of hell. In Chinese, Hindu, Buddhist, Zoroastrian, Egyptian, and Greek religious writings, eternal damnation is detailed. Christians did refine it, however, into a body of literature during the Middle Ages, using fear of eternal punishment as the stick with which to herd the flock inside Jesus's tent. Protestants contributed their share, stressing the pains of damnation and positing that the in-between of purgatory did not exist. It was all or nothing, heaven or hell forever. "Straight is the way and narrow the gate," as the gospel song has it.

Nowhere was eternal hellfire more a central tenet of belief than among those first Europeans who came to the United States. For New Englanders, the same people who executed witches on the word of Gospel preachers like Cotton Mather and his ilk, hell was a threat to be taken most seriously. Not long after Mather went to his own reward, one of Boston's most prominent ministers, Jonathan Edwards, preached a sermon called "Sinners in the Hands of an Angry God," which was reported to have brought record numbers of repentant Bostonian wrong-doers to Jesus. In it, he recounted the tortures that waited for those who did not repent: "The wrath of God burns against them, their damnation does not slumber, the pit is prepared, the fire is made ready, the furnace is now hot, ready to receive them, the flames do now rage and glow. The glittering sword is whet, and held over them, and the pit hath opened its mouth under them. Those who know not God shall have the vengeance of the flaming fire taken of them. . . ."

Hell is used more sparingly as a goad in the twenty-first century than it was in the eighteenth. "In the Middle Ages, salvation was a kind of fire insurance," said Roebuck. "I don't emphasize hell so much in my ministry, because when I read and study the life of Christ, I see a lot more grace than I do guilt. I don't see Christ strong-arming people into the Kingdom. I see him saying, there's a glorious Kingdom, there's a celebration, a banquet feast, and you're invited. You make the choice whether or not you're going to come. I don't see Christ saying, 'Come, or else I'll get you.' "

That Christ's message is one of salvation to eternal life has never been disputed among Christians. Within that given certainty, however, differences have arisen over how it will be. Will we rest eternally in the glory of God, and if so, will it be in a body of any sort, and what sort might that be? Are they the bodies we wear in this life or more perfect bodies provided us to house our souls after the Second Coming, while our earthly bodies crumble to dust forever? The Apostle Paul affirmed that we receive "spiritual" bodies, while the synoptic Gospels stressed the resurrection of the body. In fact, the physical resurrection of Jesus is the foundation on which Christianity rests, according to those disciples who knew Jesus personally, as Paul did not. It is related in Luke 24:38–39 that Jesus stood among them not long after his death, saying, "Why are ye troubled? And why do thoughts arise in your hearts?

"Behold my hands and feet, that it is I myself: handle me, and see; for a spirit have not flesh and bones, as ye see me have."

In John 11:23–26, for instance, Jesus consoles Martha when her brother, Lazarus, has died, saying: "Thy brother shall rise again."

He goes on to tell her, "I am the resurrection and the life: he that believeth in me, though he were dead, yet shall he live:

"And whosoever liveth and believeth in me shall never die."

The synoptic gospels also support the notion that those who choose *not* to believe in Jesus the Christ shall never die but will wish that they had, because they are doomed to spend eternity suffering. In Mark 9:47, Jesus admonishes: "And if thine eye offend thee, pluck it out: it is better for thee to enter into the kingdom of God with one eye, than having two eyes to be cast into hell fire . . ."

The debate about what form the resurrected body would take did not dim as the generations passed. Augustine, who lived from 354 to 430 CE, believed that the saved would eat and drink in heaven, not to sustain life but for pleasure, and that while sexual relations would not exist, men and women would appreciate each other's bodily forms for their aesthetic value. He preached a sermon in 417, according to McDannell and Lang's *Heaven: A History*, in which he said: "Take away death, the last enemy, and my own flesh will be my dear friend throughout eternity."

He is referring to flesh that is no longer corruptible, all its appetites extinguished, a return to the Edenic state of things before evil and death reared their ugly heads. The body as a creation of eternal beauty. McDannell and Lang point out that the early concept of Paradise as a garden is displaced by the growth of the medieval cities, and becomes the heavenly city where all live together in urban order and bliss. It will be a place where all shall walk naked in the forms God created. They quote from the *Elucidation*, a theological document compiled around 1100 CE, and used in many monasteries: "They will be nude, but excel in modesty, and will not blush because of any parts of their body more than they do now because of having beautiful eyes."

A vision worth dying for, so to speak. The Crusades provided the perfect opportunity to do so, as well as an excellent means of thinning out the younger male population, thereby relieving a source of pressure on available resources. For those who traveled off to the holy wars, it was the luck of the draw. Some arrived back home safe, sound, and prosperous. For many others, while they might return as poor and prospectless as they were before they left, at least they had eaten every day in exchange for their service in the Lord's army. But many died in foreign lands, their bodies laid down in alien ground forever. For them, full penance and an immediate ticket to Paradise was guaranteed in return for having paid the ultimate price in the Crusades.

In earlier Christian centuries, martyrdom had served the same purpose—an instant ticket to eternal life. To die for Christ was to win eternity with Him. It could happen in a lot of ways, and they are explained saint by saint in *Lives of the Saints*, an exhaustive catalog of the persecutions to which Christians were liable. Sometime before the Middle Ages began, a shift happened. Christians no longer risked their lives by professing faith in Christ but by going out to wage war against the heathen in His name. Tens of thousands joined up to slaughter Jews and Muslims in far-off lands. Armies of the Lord. To die on a battlefield, having killed or murdered as many nonbelievers as possible, was the equivalent of choosing death rather than renouncing Christian principles. Paradise awaited. In 1095, Pope Urban II said that those who died on the battlefield of the First Crusade would receive plenary indulgence and full absolution of their sins. They would, in other words, go straight to Paradise and immortal life.

This would bypass the vexing problem of purgatory, that in-between and unpleasant stopping place of so many souls after death. The souls in purgatory were at the mercy of the living they left behind, who were the only ones who could pray and pay souls along toward heaven. In the Middle Ages, the Church sold indulgences, which reduced a soul's time in purgatory. The sale or purchase of indulgences was banned by the Council of Trent in 1562.

While indulgences are no longer for sale the Vatican, purgatory continues to be one of the ingredients in the Roman Catholic recipe for what happens after we die. "Part of official Catholic doctrine, purgatory is a condition (rather than a place) of transition and adaptation for those entering heavenly beatitude, a passage at once painful and joyful into purified fullness of life with God," writes Catholic theologian Francis Cleary in an essay in *How Different Religions View Death and Afterlife.*

Prohibiting the sale of indulgences was a case of shutting the barn door after the horse had gotten out. The greed and corrupt behavior of the papacy regarding indulgences had already pushed Martin Luther beyond the breaking point and thereby helped to initiate the Reformation. Protestants rejected purgatory and all its trappings out of hand. It will be heaven or hell, they insisted. A judgment waited after death that would award eternity in heaven or condemn the recently deceased to spend forever in the fires of hell. It was a frightening idea, particularly for those living where the plague struck, as it did frequently in the times of the Protestant Reformation. Life, ever uncertain, was much more precarious when the plague arrived. People who were in perfectly good health fell ill and died in terribly quick time. Practically from one moment to the next, the well fell down sick and dying. These were years when whole cities took ill, when the dead were piled up in the streets to be hauled to the boneyard. Life in such a place seemed very short; eternity, very long.

Explanations were in short supply in plague-stricken cities, science was powerless in the face of the disease, doctors' skills failed utterly. No one imagined that fleas might transmit the disease. It was, however, easily imaginable that the plague was God's hand reaching down to wipe the slate clean. It appeared as an inexorable force. Take the outbreak of plague in Barcelona in 1651. The Barcelonese had watched in mounting panic as thousands died in Valencia, 150 miles to the south, in 1649. By 1650, the plague had reached Tarragona, only 50 miles away.

The highways into Barcelona were virtually closed to travelers from the plague areas, according to James Amelang's book *A Journal of the Plague Year*, his translation of the journal of a Barcelona tanner named Miquel Parets, written in Catalan. In it, the tanner records how desperate municipal authorities turned to prayer as the plague continued its implacable march north toward them from the south. "The city of Barcelona ordered its monasteries and convents to say prayers for protection against the plague and to display the Holy Sacrament in all the churches, beginning with the Cathedral and then the monasteries and parish churches one by one. Processions were held, and prayers were said to placate the anger of Our Lord God."

It did no good at all in forestalling the arrival of the disease, which reached the city just after New Year in the winter of 1651. The plague would carry off a third of the population, some fifteen thousand people. The tanner wrote of the dimensions of the Lord's wrath, "There are no words to describe the prayers and processions carried out in Barcelona, and the crowds of penitents and young girls with crosses who marched through the city saying their devotions. The streets were constantly full of people, many greatly devout and carrying candles and crying out 'Lord God, have mercy!' . . . But Our Lord was so angered by our sins that the more processions were carried out the more the plague spread."

Faced with a daily reality of family and friends sickening and dying, it was no surprise that many became convinced that the last days were approaching. It was not a new idea. The very beginnings of Christianity are rooted in the belief that the end was nigh, the Apostles were convinced that the Apocalypse was up on them, that they were living in the last years. They were the first of a long line of Christians to dance the Apocalypso Calypso, and proclaim with certainty that their generation was the last one. Even in those eras in which no virulent disease wipes out great swathes of the world's population, there is always some sect somewhere with members who are convinced by their readings of the New Testament that the last days have arrived. To prove their complete faith in that notion, they often jump the gun, go off the rails, blow themselves up, or do themselves in. Of course, Christians have no monopoly on that sort of behavior. At bottom, the Apocalyse-Now conviction is an excessive reaction against death, the belief that if I am going to die shortly, the world must also be at the brink of extinction. Despite millennia of assertions that human history is about to end, it has not happened yet. This has not prevented the eruption here and there in every generation of sects who believe the end times are near.

In our own times, members of groups like the People's Temple in Jonestown, Guyana, the Order of the Solar Temple near Geneva, Switzerland, and the members of Southern California's Heaven's Gate all have been willing participants in collective suicides. In each instance, members followed a person whom the press inevitably described as a "charismatic personality" into the hinterlands of death. "When the Solar Temple adepts decided that the world's population was stubbornly refusing to transform to create the Age of Aquarius, they shifted their expectation of terrestrial salvation to an otherworldly realm, to which they made several group 'transits' by murder and group suicide," writes Catherine Wessinger in *How the Millennium Comes Violently.*

Heaven's Gate adepts were convinced they were bound for a new world. "Ultimately they abandoned their human bodies, their terrestrial 'vehicles,' confident that their souls were transferred into divinized extraterrestrial bodies," Wessinger writes. "They exited Earth in 1997 (they did not regard this as suicide), because catastrophic destruction was imminent due to an overgrowth of evil here in this 'garden.'"

Now, at the beginning of the twenty-first century, the suicide bombers of the Islamic fundamentalist groups in Bagdhad, London, Gaza, and New York are shining examples of people convinced that death is not to be feared because following their heroic deaths, they shall immediately wake up in a paradise worth dying for. What they have really died for is to gain a moment's attention, a blip on a global map of dying for a cause, a media sensation for a day. Beyond this, they believe that unending pleasure and closeness to the sacred await them in the next world. Peace and beautiful maidens will be their portion when they next open their eyes, after blowing themselves up in this world to strike at a heathen enemy.

Islam, when it appeared in the seventh century CE, incorporated many aspects of both Christianity and Judaism, but it also created a distinctive world order ruled by one God and illuminated through the words of a prophet his followers believed to be greater than Moses or Jesus, an illiterate, enlightened teacher named Mohammed. Islamic belief is that Jews, Christians, and Muslims are all "People of the Book," but that Mohammed's message is the last word. Like the Orthodox Jews and the Christians before him, Mohammed taught an eschatology—what people think happens after death—of resurrection, judgment, and eternal life in a body, in either heaven or hell. Unlike Christians and Jews, little or no division of opinion exists as to whether this will be in a "spiritual" body or in one's own resurrected physical body. Almost all Muslims opt for the latter. People in Paradise will spend their days in delight, drinking milk and honey, eating the finest fruits with flavors of unimaginable richness, their evenings enriched by the presence of the loveliest of beings. Heaven is unending pleasure enjoyed in one's own perfect body.

Entrance into Paradise is preceded by two judgments,

one shortly after death and one at the Resurrection. Every person shall be judged on the thoughts and actions of a lifetime. Many will not make it, even those who profess the faith, and they shall accompany the infidels into hell. The damned have it every bit as bad in hell as the blessed have it good in Paradise, and it is just as much a physical experience. The flames of hell are hotter than anything we can imagine, excruciating pain everlasting, fueled by human bodies and stones. Every time a person's body is burnt up, a new one is created, and eternity is spent in this fashion, in the most extreme agony. Instead of drinking from Paradise's rivers of milk and honey, hell's inhabitants will have to quench their thirsts with pus.

A first judgment is rendered shortly after death when the newly dead are visited in the grave by two angels, Munkar and Nakir. They quiz the dead person on articles of faith, and those who answer correctly—unwaveringly and unhesitatingly—receive a favorable verdict. They will wait comfortably in their graves for Resurrection Day, but those who receive a damning verdict will endure pain and suffering in their graves, the "first chastisement." Then, at some point in the future known only to Allah, the Resurrection will come and every soul that has lived shall be judged, answering for thoughts and actions. "This moment is the occasion of enormous elaboration in later Muslim tradition," writes Alan Segal. "People are reclothed in flesh and sit on the grave waiting for their verdict."

The dead shall have to cross a bridge, virtually the same

bridge found in Zoroastrian thought, and be judged on their thoughts and deeds as recorded in the holy book, the same holy book of life with all the records of all the righteous who ever lived that we find in Judaism, the same book that will be opened on the Christian Day of Judgment and Resurrection. Yet, for all the ways in which it has evidently drawn on the monotheisms that preceded it, Islamic afterlife is quite distinct.

"There are seven levels of Paradise, and the highest is the seventh level," Awadh Binhazim, a board member of the Nashville Islamic center, explained to me. "The levels of pleasure, entertainment, and felicity increase as the numbers go higher.

"Even at the lowest level, none of what we have seen on earth can even start to describe what is waiting for us there. If you get to even the first level, you're going to be okay," he chuckled, a slight edge of anticipation in his laugh. "You're going to be *quite* okay."

Binhazim, forty-four, is a trim, neat man with a Middle Eastern tone to his dark skin and straight, short, salt-and-pepper hair, a groomed goatee, and mustache. A pathologist who teaches at Meharry Medical College in Nashville, he wears gray, steel-rimmed glasses and has a serious, learned mien. He has attended his share of autopsies and knows his way around the human body.

What determines the level of paradise a person reaches, Benhazim told me, is first his or her life, with its good deeds and righteous ways, but also how much of the Qur'an a person can recite. "Once you have been destined to be a person of Paradise you'll be told, 'Paradise is your destination. Arise and ascend and recite.' Where you stop reciting will be the level where you'll be. People who have memorized the entire Qur'an, and there are many, will reach a higher level.

"Many pleasures and pleasant experiences await us in Paradise. One of those is the sexual experience that people will enjoy at that time. If they qualify to get into Paradise there will be an experience of meeting these incredibly beautiful women who live in Paradise. However, a married person will be with his wife, except that the wife is said to have more beauty than these beautiful maidens who are in Paradise. Naturally, a man will prefer his wife."

Benhazim was born and raised in Kenya and has lived in Nashville for seven years, having come to the States to attend medical school at the University of Georgia and stayed on. When he arrived in Nashville in 1998, the city had thirteen thousand Muslims and two mosques. By 2005, the population had grown to twenty thousand, enough to support four mosques. Kurds, Somalis, and people from other African and Middle Eastern countries continued arriving in substantial numbers. When journalists and others from the non-Islamic Nashville community have a question about the faith, they are often steered to Awadh Binhazim.

"Certain features of paradise are simply unimaginable to us. For example, the Qur'an talks of one tree. It says, 'We will admit you into gardens with shade never-ending.' The exegetes of the Qur'an have studied that further and know from the experience of the prophet when he was taken to be shown paradise that if a man on horseback set off from that tree and rode continuously for one hundred years he would not reach the end of the shade of this tree. From here to the distance of the moon and back is covered by the shade of that one tree. How can we comprehend such a concept? We cannot. Our minds are finite, not infinite, and we will be dealing in Paradise with what is infinite.

"That's why there is a teaching in the Qur'an where Allah says, 'I have prepared for my righteous servants that which no eye has ever seen and that which no ear has ever heard and that which no heart could even comprehend.'"

This echoes Paul in 1 Corinthians 2:9, where it is written: "But as it is written, Eye hath not seen, nor ear heard, neither have entered into the heart of man, the things which God hath prepared for them that love him"; a verse that in turn refers to Isaiah 64:4: "For since the beginning of the world men have not heard, nor perceived by the ear, neither hath the eye seen, O God, beside thee, what he hath prepared for him that waiteth for him."

The same formula for immortal life is repeated in the monotheisms down through the centuries: attune the heart and actions to the one God, and life everlasting in a resurrected body will be the reward. Each person is a unique individual whose deeds are recorded in the book of life and judged. It is a powerful doctrine that has attracted billions of people since Zarathustra first brought the message. It is an impressively broad and deep vein of belief that runs all the way through the Resurrection faiths, from Zoroastrianism into Judaism and Christianity, then into Islam. All these billions of people bound by a common assurance that they will be resurrected, able to live again and recognize their loved ones. Experienced from inside any given historical moment, through the lens of any one individual's life and religious beliefs, the Resurrection faith may seem to have fractured and splintered into groups like Orthodox, Conservative, and Reform; or Catholic, Baptist, and Church of Christ; or Sunni, Shiite, and Sufi. Viewed from the banks of history, however, Jews, Christians, Muslims, and Zoroastrians all hold the same faith; it's the same river flowing by, the same belief informing so many billions of lives over the course of millennia, the same conviction that once created, we shall live again.

Not so long ago, the empirical sciences were like boulders in this river, a set of observable truths obstructing the smooth flow of belief and apparently disproving the possibility that a body could live again. Yet in our brief lifetimes we have watched the basic building blocks of all bodies brought to light, investigative science at its best revealing the inner workings of the machine. The book of life has been opened, scientists tell us, and its alphabet deciphered. It only remains for investigators to learn how to write the language effectively. Once they understand how to do that, it may be possible to defeat death or at least to live so long that death's sting is greatly reduced. Stem cells, telomere research, and nanotechnology are becoming as much a part of the twenty-first-century discourse about resurrection and immortality as the Bible or the Qur'an.

PART TWO
The Soul Moves On

Cow patties drying on a ghat in the sun. Varanasi, India. *Courtesy of Heiko Bennewitz, iStockphoto.*

3

Another Time Around

After all, it is no more surprising to be born twice than it is to be born once.

From Voltaire

The second category of belief about life after death holds that a dead body is left behind to molder while the soul that inhabited it lives on, an animated, exalted bit of essence we all carry within us, stamped and shaped by our individual lives and choices, which survives our physical forms. It is a belief held in some form or another by people as diverse as Buddhists, Hindus, New Agers, Roman Catholics, trance mediums, Taoists, some Jews, and independent believers of many stripes.

Belief in a soul requires every bit as much faith as believing in a body that will be resurrected to live forever. The soul's existence is no more or less certain than the resurrected body's. An urban legend has it that the body loses weight when it dies, and that this loss is the soul leaving. In the early 1900s, a Massachusetts physician named Duncan McDougal built a special frame bed/scale on which to place his moribund patients. He was able to obtain weights for four of them immediately following death and noted they lost between three-eighths and three-quarters of an ounce, according to a report on the Internet at www.snopes.com. The three-quarters of an ounce was the largest weight loss he found for humans. In his March 1907 article for *American Medicine*, McDougal wrote: "In this case we certainly have an inexplicable loss of weight of three-quarters of an ounce. Is it the soul substance? How other shall we explain it?"

Subsequently, he weighed fifteen dogs at the moment he put them to death, and found no variation in the pre- and post-mortem states. Mary Roach reports in her book, *Spook:Science Tackles the Afterlife* that McDougal claimed this finding made sense, because animals have no souls. His experiments remain unconfirmed. No one in the history of this world has produced irrefutable evidence proving the existence of a soul. On the other hand, many people at some moment during their lives have felt something about themselves that seemed more than the sum of flesh and blood and biochemistry. Beyond this point of agreement, however, the soul's trajectory after death is the subject of many different interpretations around the world.

One of the oldest is reincarnation. Its ancient history is rooted in Hindu eschatology stretching back thousands of years. Hinduism, as the British named it in the 1800s, and Vedanta or Brahmanism or Sanatana Dharma (the eternal way), as its practitioners have called it, is one of the world's most ancient religions, born and developed in India and shared by vast numbers of people over millennia. Currently it has 750 million followers around the world. The development of Hindu thought about reincarnation, as about virtually everything else, can be traced through its sacred literature. The first of the holy texts, the Vedas (*veda* means "wisdom" or "vision" in Sanskrit), were written as long ago as 3000 BCE, according to some researchers. The first texts consists of four Vedas, each a collection of material including ritual incantations and instructions, and they basically deal with how to worship in the here-and-now world—how to conduct oneself in daily life.

The Upanishads, written between 700 and 100 BCE, refine the concepts of reincarnation and the law of karma, illuminating this life and the world to come for believers. They describe the endless turning of the wheel of samsara in each of our lives, the wheel of birth and death to which each of our souls is bound, born to die and be born again in another of the world's 8.4 million possible life forms, passing through centuries of lives, slowly working off old mistakes. "As a man leaves an old garment and puts on one that is new, the Spirit leaves its mortal body and puts on one that is new," according to the Bhagavad Gita, a book within the Upanishads so loved by Hindus that it is sometimes called the fifth Veda.

The new body referred to in the Gita, however, is not the immortal spiritual body that Paul will guarantee some centuries later to the Corinthians. The Hindu scripture is referring to a new flesh-bone-and-blood body, a seemingly endless succession of them. This is not immortality but an apparently interminable series of rebirths into one suffering life after another. The soul yearns to rejoin the original divine nature from which it emanated. It is to this that Hindus aspire, this dissolution of the individual, *moksha*, this liberation from physical life, an end to rebirth and suffering, and a return to the immortal essence of all beings.

This goal of liberation from the endless cycle of rebirths, samsara, is as difficult to achieve for most Hindus as sainthood is for your average Roman Catholic. Instead, what awaits is rebirth into lives whose qualities will be defined by the law of karma. In the next life, we shall reap what we have sown in this one and in those past. "According to the doctrine of karma, all actions—sinful or meritorious— are held to have more or less inevitable consequences which the actor will harvest in this or future lives," writes Jonathan Parry in *Death in Banaras.*

The entire process by which karma operates is complex, with a variety of possibilities for a soul following death that include time spent in hell or roaming the world as a hungry ghost. Escaping the cycle of death and rebirth is supremely difficult but not impossible. One way to make it easier is through devotion to a deity. Many Westerners assume, erroneously, that Hinduism is a polytheistic religion, but Hindus consider themselves monotheistic. All gods and everything else sacred, including our own souls, come from a single divine source. Hindus will devote themselves to one of the deities, such as Krishna, or Shiva, or Ganesh, hoping for assistance and focus in obtaining knowledge of the divine and so eternal reunification with it. Each deity has his or her own road to the sacred.

Another way to end the cycle of birth and death is to die in India's holiest city, currently called Varanasi, formerly named Banaras by the British, and known as well by its more ancient name, Kashi, meaning the city of light. Located in northeastern India, it is called Varanasi because it is built alongside the Ganges River between two of its tributaries, the Varuna and the Asi rivers. It is among the oldest inhabited cities on earth, according to almost everybody, and Brahmanic tradition holds that it is the city where the world began, that its origins precede time itself. "Its present life reaches back to the sixth century BCE in a continuous tradition," writes Diana Eck in her book, *Banaras: City of*

Light. "If we could imagine the silent Acropolis and the Agora of Athens still alive with the intellectual, cultural, and ritual traditions of classical Greece, we might glimpse the remarkable tenacity of life in Kashi. Today Peking, Athens, and Jerusalem are moved by a very different ethos from that which moved them in ancient times, but Kashi is not."

To die here, to have one's ashes scattered in the sacred Ganges, is to assure *moksha*, to guarantee the liberation of the soul from the cycle of rebirth. The river originates hundreds of miles to the north in the high Himalayas, but when it reaches the large bend where Varanasi stands, the Ganges curves so dramatically that it flows by the city south to north. Everything is special about Kashi, and it has been ever thus. It is a city of death and eternal life, where dying is not to be feared nor mourned, but welcomed. "Kashi is as old as time itself," writes Parry. "As the site of cosmic creation, it is the place where time itself began. As cosmogony is here a ceaselessly repeated event, its present time is also the primordial time of origins.

"It is the city's association with death that provides it with an immunity to the degenerative flow of time, and renews its capacity to encompass the rest of creation."

It is also an overcrowded, dirty city of 1.2 million people who use open gutters alongside their narrow streets for toilets and toss their garbage outside for cows, water buffalo, goats, and dogs to spend their days rooting through. Barefoot, unschooled children follow the bovines, recovering their dung, which their families will dry and use as fuel.

Varanasi has a couple of foggy, cool months, but mostly it is hot and dusty. Extremely dusty, except when the monsoons are falling, and then it's muddy. It is a city packed well beyond the bursting point with vehicular traffic. The potholed broken streets belong primarily to the animals, but they share them with the private cars of the well-to-do and doing-well, motor scooters, motorcycles, huge numbers of three-wheeled auto rickshaws powered by diesel or gasoline, and bicycle rickshaws powered by the stringy muscles of a pair of legs often as past their prime as my own. All these conveyances are constantly sounding their horns and ringing their bells, careening and swerving, trying to clear a space ahead to squeeze through, launching themselves toward an occupied space in the certainty that when they arrive it will be empty. To go from one point in Varanasi to another in any sort of vehicle is a trip not likely to be soon forgotten.

The city's air has a toxic consistency. Breathing it leaves grit on the teeth, and the holy river is asked to absorb far more than its fair share of abuse. A half-dozen species of fish lived in the waters of the Ganges alongside Varanasi fifty years ago, but today only catfish are caught there, and in ever-shrinking numbers, according to local fishmongers. Electricity is a precious commodity and usually only functions after 4:00 P.M. This is particularly tough in a crowded of dusty city where temperatures reach 120°F during the hottest months. People live in large numbers in small spaces. Yet the city is full of sudden quiet alleyways opening up into the thoroughfares, people living in one small room after another along narrow lanes hardly wide enough for a cow to amble down, an open space behind the houses where they can spend the night on rope beds in the cooler air outside.

From my hotel I look down on a roof where every afternoon three women in colorful saris appear. They hang laundry, then lounge around on mats in the shade of the drying saris and shirts, laughing away a pair of hours, while their kids fly kites from the rooftop. In Varanasi, boys fly kites the way they play soccer in Barcelona or shoot baskets in Nashville—anywhere and everywhere, for hours. At any time of day, over any spot in the city, small rhomboid, tailless kites are fluttering and swooping, rising and dipping against the sky.

Kashi's sacred status is the city's largest industry. Pilgrims arrive constantly—over a million of them visit annually, according to Parry. Estimates are that some 75 percent of jobs in the city are connected in some way to their comings and goings. Additionally, death is a huge business in Kashi. Life and death along the vast stone steps coming down to the river's edge, the more than one hundred ghats of Kashi, are as ancient as urban life anywhere. Nothing is more holy than cremation on one of Kashi's two burning ghats: Manikarnika ghat or Harischandra ghat. Day and night bodies are burned, the pyres of wood tended by Untouchables as the dead person's relatives watch impassively. Nothing is more desirable than to die between the Varuna and Asi rivers. Traffic is frequently complicated by a procession of people moving down a main street behind four men bearing a bamboo ladder on their shoulders, along the length of which is stretched a body wrapped in white and covered with gold and silver foil paper, headed for one of the two burning ghats. Beneath the deadweight on their shoulders, the bearers chant over and over again, "*Ram-nam sat hai*" ("Truth is in the name of Ram").

To provide the rituals and trappings of a good death in Varanasi requires a substantial expense on the part of the deceased's family. The ashes are then swept into the river. The bodies of those dead whose families cannot afford cremation are sometimes dumped directly into the river, and while the body may slowly decompose in the water, the soul goes directly to the place from which it arose, off the wheel at last. Meanwhile, Varanasi's teeming living use the Ganges for bathing, washing, drinking, and swimming.

My own arrival at Varanasi in the fall of 2005 was on a highly auspicious day, according to the young man with whom—along with his mother, wife, and sister-in-law—I shared a compartment on the four-hundred-mile, fourteen-hour trip from Delhi southeast to Varanasi on the evening express. I had slept better than expected on the fold-away ironing board that served as a sleeping platform in second class. I opened my eyes to morning outside the train, passing through flatlands, a couple of hours from Varanasi. The first thing I saw when I looked out was an image framed by the train window that imprinted on my memory: a shallow, scummy, small pool of dark standing water in front of a mud-brick hut, a single pink lotus in bloom in the middle of that evil-looking liquid.

The guy on the train was from Vanarasi and was on his way home; he told me it was the day of Dev Diwali, the festival of light held on the full moon in the Hindu month of Kartika, which spans October and November. It is the first full moon following the Hindu celebration of Diwali, the new year. To arrive in Vanarasi on Dev Diwali, he explained, was an excellent sign. Indeed, that evening the ghats along the riverside were alight with wicks burning in small clay bowls of oil lined up along the steps. The ghats were covered in candlelight. Little round vessels constructed of leaves were set floating on the river, a lit wick in each, and they twinkled along the surface. Bells rang, drums were played, the gods were welcomed and guided by the lights.

The city's population is estimated at around 80 percent Hindu, some 15 to 20 percent of whom are Brahmans, highly religious and conservative on questions like caste and how to treat the minority Muslim population. Banaras Vanarasi is home to more than twelve hundred temples, ranging from the grand Golden Temple, constructed with three-quarters of a ton of gold in 1776, to innumerable small shrines on street corners that have room to admit only one person at a time to a god's image and presence, where a person can offer obeisance and a wreath of marigolds and accumulate merit. As Nashville is to the Bible Belt, so Kashi is to India, a city with a church or temple on every corner, a student of the Scriptures behind the wheel of every taxi or pedaling every rickshaw.

Ashrams are scattered throughout Kashi—monasteries where the sanyassin live, those who have renounced everything. They have died to their old lives, whatever they may have been, and live only in the faith. Hindus believe life divides into four parts, each with different responsibilities. The last stage of life, when a person's children are out and on their own and householder duties are fulfilled, is a time to renounce the world as known for sixty or so years and take up a life focused on developing the soul. For many, that means liquidating their assets and moving to Kashi to contemplate, study, bathe each day in the waters of Mother Ganga (pronounced *ghan-ga*), the Ganges River, and prepare for death in the holy city.

Behind my hotel was a three-story ashram dedicated to one Sri Devahara Baba, with some forty sanyassin residing in small rooms at any one time. Mornings and evenings they celebrated their daily praise worship with bells and drums and chanting in a large, ground-level, central hall with marble floors and a black marble statue of Vishnu. At other times, the ashram was deeply quiet, a silence often pierced by the lowing of one of the three cows in residence in a stable in another part of the ground floor; there was a huge pile of cow manure in a corner and the entire building had a background smell of cow barn.

"No one has died and come back to inform us about what happened, so whatever proof we have about what happens after death is what we find in the Scriptures," said Swami Ram Balak, the ashram's guru, whose own guru had preceded him here. He was a compact man who gave his age as over seventy and who sat on a small bench cross-legged and straight-backed, slightly above where I sat with a translator on woven mats at his feet. A weak naked bulb in a socket high on the wall gave us enough light to see each other amidst shadows. Mosquitoes came and went through the light like dust motes. The swami told us he had lived there over fifty years.

Gray tufts of hair curled out from beneath the edge of his saffron turban. He had a broad nose, a penetrating gaze, and a strong face. "According to Scripture, Lord Shiva will give liberation to all who die in Kashi. I'm here, living as I do, to prepare for that. Everyone wants *moksha* for themselves, I'm no different. But it's in the hand of God. With the grace of God we shall succeed and achieve liberation. It's like a university exam where a person fails or passes. If they fail, they study more and take the exam again. The same for liberation. If they fail in this life, they'll try again. I'm trying to live in such a way as to get it in this life, but God decides."

When the time comes, Ram Balak-ji will not need to be cremated, because sanyassin have already died when they renounced the world. They need only be wrapped in a cloth, weighted down, and immersed in the Ganges. Like-wise, the bodies of babies under nine months old are wrapped and sunk. But whether their dead and done bodies are returned to the river as ashes or as flesh on bone, it will be a last bath in the same holy river that washed and nurtured them while they lived. Those without the karma to have been born in Kashi with those waters to hand on a daily basis try to come at least once in their lives to pay their respects to Mother Ganga. At sunrise, the ghats are crowded with pilgrims who have come to bathe in her waters and city residents who have scraped together a little something to eat and moved on to getting through the day. The *chai* stalls open, selling their sweetened milk-tea, the national drink; the streets get crowded and loud with the day's business, with horns honking, bells ringing, and by midmorning six bodies will be burning at Manikarnika ghat and another six at Harischandra, with a couple more in each place waiting, wrapped in cloth on bamboo stretchers by the water's edge, where a dozen kids frolic in the river, men wearing loincloths are bent over brushing their teeth, others soap themselves and dive in for a morning wash, and women in saris are already scrubbing piles of clothes.

I lean on an iron railing and watch the fires at Manikarnika, perhaps the most sacred place in Varanasi, where Vishnu is said to have created the world. Diane Eck names it as the most important ghat in Kashi and adds, "It is said to be the place of the earth's creation as well as its destruction, containing both the sacred well, dug out by Vishnu at the beginning of time, and the cremation ground, where the created order burns at the end of time."

The Untouchable in charge of the burning this morning pokes with a long bamboo pole at the pyre of what appears to have been an older man, by the charred remains. An arm falls off, hand clawed; the Untouchable pokes it back into the flames. After a moment, he calls to the "chief mourner," traditionally the deceased's oldest son, who is dressed in a simple white cloth dhoti, with his skull shaved and a small topknot of hair. The Untouchable leads him to the fire—it is his job to know when to do this—and hands the long bamboo pole to the son, pointing at a place in the flames. This chief mourner, a middle-aged, slightly paunchy man, looks somewhat queasy but resolute. With the pole, he whacks the skull of his burning father three times until it cracks. This is done to let the dead person's vital spirit escape and is perhaps the most important moment in the cremation process. The son tosses the pole to the ground and moves away, seemingly glad to do so.

Beside this body is burning another—the blackened shell of a younger man. He had a black beard, which is curling up and disappearing his lower legs and feet hang over the pyre of crisscrossed logs, a charred stump of a penis, the outline of a person behind blackened skin. The smoke is dense and the flames make a fatty crackle, but the smell is not as bad as I had expected. The Untouchables who do the burning make a good living and they go about their work with care and expertise. It is a skill passed on from father to son, as are many of the ancillary industries generated by death in Varanasi.

A body must be cremated within twenty-four hours of death and generally takes about three hours to burn. The price for the cremation will be based on a complicated formula involving the deceased's weight and how much wood will be needed, plus an additional sum added on according to what the family can bear, a negotiation familiar to an Egyptian priest in 1000 BCE or a funeral home director in the twenty-first century CE. It will not be cheap. Wood grows steadily scarcer and more expensive around the city, and cremation prices continue to rise. Despite the high prices, business at the burning ghats is always brisk. People who can, come to die in Kashi. Many times a family will come from a smaller village in the surrounding countryside with someone who is dying. If they are poor, they can use one of two hospices in Kashi maintained by charitable organizations, where relatives can stay with the dying person through the process, then have the body cremated beside the Ganga if they can afford it. If not, at least loved ones have died in Kashi, and their roads to *moksha* will be much shorter for it.

One such hospice, located at Manikarnika ghat, was estimated in Christopher Justice's book *Dying the Good Death* to have received around ten thousand people who came to die over the course of sixty years. Yet another, close to Asi ghat, is more of an "assisted living" facility where a person pays a substantial sum for a room in which to age and die. A third is the Kashi Labh Muktibhavan. Located behind a high wall along which monkeys occasionally scamper, it is close to the intersection of Church and Godowlia streets, two of the busiest streets in Banaras and therefore two of the most chaotic in the world. Once one is inside the Muktibhavan's gate, however, the sounds of the city virtually disappear. Four priests live in small rooms at the back, and their work is chanting in two-hour shifts into a microphone that broadcasts to each of the ten rooms set aside for dying people. Each room has a raised wooden pallet, a stone shelf, and a small, barred window. Family members arrive with the dying person and stay with them in the room. Toward the front of the building is a large, bare room set aside for the families to use as a common room.

People are brought here in the last stages of death. They have almost always stopped eating by the time they arrive and are likely slipping in and out of consciousness. They take in no nourishment other than twice a day when they are given a bit of water from the Ganga and a tulsa leaf, a kind of wild basil considered sacred. If they do not die within two weeks, their families must ask for permission to stay longer and will be sent home if people are waiting for admission. In his book, Justice recorded that from mid-1990 to mid-1991, 365 people came to the Muktibhavan to die, of whom 305 did so. Numbers are down since then, however, and when I visited, no *rogi marnewalas* (dying people) were on the premises. The last person had improved enough to go back to her village only that morning.

The hospice is administered by Bhairavnath Shukla, and he has had the job for over twenty-three years. He is small, thin, a brown-skinned man with a thin, gray mustache and close-cut gray hair. I asked him if he was bothered by overseeing so much death. "This is not a depressing job," he answered, breaking into a cough, an affliction shared by nearly everyone who spends much time in this dusty city. "The people come here to leave their souls and they are not sad about it, so why should I be? This is a good work. My family and I are blessed. These are people who have come here to die and receive *moksha*, so we feel happy just to serve them.

"Rich people can afford to come live out their last years in Kashi and wait to die, but poor people can't do this. When the family feels the last days have come to a loved one, they can bring that person here."

Unless, of course, they should happen to be a family from an Untouchable caste, in which case, said Shukla-ji, there are other places in Kashi designated to care for them—the hospice at Manikarnika ghat, for instance. Things must be kept calm and supportive at the Muktibhavan. No card playing is allowed among family members, and frivolity of any sort is not acceptable behavior. Things are serious, but not depressing, he said. People are accepting of what is happening. "Family members are not grieving when they are here. Of course we miss our mothers, our fathers, our sons, and our daughters when they die, but we have had a thousand mothers, a thousand fathers, a thousand sons, a thousand daughters since when the *kaliyuga*, this phase of time, began. We have been reborn many times."

Shukla-ji said that his years spent at the Muktibhavan had made his belief in rebirth all the stronger. "Working here has convinced me that the soul is immortal. It doesn't die.

It just changes its clothes, it just changes bodies, but the soul is immortal. There's no need worry about clothes. We get them dirty and wash them, they get torn and we mend them, but eventually we throw them away. That's what people here are doing."

Where those "old clothes" often get tossed away is into the Ganges, and boatmen play a key role in the process. When a body is disposed of in the river, a boatman receives a negotiated price for taking the living and the dead out, and bringing the living back. The boatmen at the ghats are organized into shifts, with someone always on duty. Their most frequent calls are to row the weighted bodies of babies to the middle of the river, where a father will consign the infant to the Ganga's depths. "Mine might sound like a sad job to someone from somewhere else, but it's not," a twenty-year-old boatman named Vinod Sahani told me. "This job is providing an important service. When someone has died, the death ritual must be performed. Adults need to be cremated, and babies and sanyassins need to be immersed."

He is short, with a wandering left eye, dark skin, a thin mustache, hair combed wet to one side, and even, white teeth that gleam when he smiles, which is frequently while we speak. At least five generations of his family have been boatmen here. His father has a turn on the immersion shift at Manikarnika ghat. His mother lives in a village not far from Varanasi with his three sisters. She is poor, and the girls will need money to marry. He had to leave school at the age of thirteen to come to the city and work with his father, who has an unfortunate liking for strong drink. "It's a survival wage, but it's hard work," he said. "I get here at six A.M., and work until seven P.M. Some days there is no business. I would like to have continued my studies, but I had to come here."

I hire him to bring myself and the Hindi translator back upriver to Asi ghat, where I am staying. As we are getting into his boat, a man appears at the top of the ghat, a tight-wrapped, small, white bundle in his arms. He is dressed in a simple white kurta. An air of dignified, deep sorrow is around the man, his hands cradling the little shrouded body, which is no longer than his forearm. Vinod Sahani goes up the steps to talk with him and get him squared away with another boatman.

Sahani's boat is about fifteen feet long, a curving, water-tight vessel of wooden planks with mismatched oars and rope oarlocks. He is rowing at a strong pace against the current. Halfway back we pass a waterlogged something not ten yards away, a swollen, sodden mass of bloated and flyblown flesh. It drifts by quickly, bobbing in the current. Sahani glances briefly at the mottled form as it goes by. "A male," he says. "Forty-five to fifty years old. The bodies drift down from villages where they are tossed into the Ganges because people are too poor to bring them to Kashi."

In theory, the police are responsible for collecting the bodies from the river, attempting to identify them, and cremating them in the city's electric crematorium, a huge incinerating facility that was inaugurated in 1986 in the hope that it would provide the poor an alternative to tossing bodies in the river. Unfortunately, it is rarely in operation. Electricity works in Varanasi for only about twelve hours a day. In addition, it is thought that the heavily government-subsidized crematorium raised the ire of those around the ghats who make their living from private cremations. A series of mysterious breakdowns has crippled the facility for long periods of time. Whatever the reasons, the municipal crematorium stands idle and empty, a concrete hulk on the riverside. As if this was not reason enough to discourage the police from performing their legal obligation to recover and identify the bodies, the floaters are not pleasant to handle, says Sahani. Their smell is hard to wash off, and they are deemed highly impure, so they are often left in the water to drift through one jurisdiction to the next, until finally they either cross the Varuna and leave Varanasi or decompose into the water.

Catfish, anyone?

I watch a single boat, packed to the gunwales with passengers, slowly, slowly cross the river with long, broad sweeps of its oars; the boat moves so slowly that it leaves no wake behind. It makes the far shore, the vast, barren expanse of sand across the Ganges from Varanasi, where people sometimes go to picnic or fish or bathe but where no one wants to die, because to die on that side of the river is believed to result inevitably in rebirth as a donkey.

A belief in rebirth of the soul after death is not limited to the world's 750 million Hindus. The estimated 500 million Buddhists on earth also expect to be reborn. It is not surprising that Buddhism's concept of the afterlife should be similar, because it is a religion that grew out of Hinduism. Siddhartha Gautama, who was born a Hindu (as Jesus was born a Jew), would become the Buddha when, at the age of twenty-nine, he understood with his whole being why we are born and why we die—that we are all equal in our attachment to suffering. In Buddhism, there are no gods and there are no castes. Rebirth is a cross, not a comfort, suffering is the energy that turns the wheel of the world, and after people have passed through eons of lifetimes, they can hope to become enlightened and wholly compassionate and to end their cycle of involuntary return.

It is all right. There is time. No hurry. Another thing that Buddhism and Hinduism share is a sense of vast universal time, of the transient nature of the world and all the forms it takes, of its minuscule importance in the larger scheme of things. Hindu mythology tells how Brahma, the creator, creates the material world over and over in lifetimes that last a hundred divine years. Each day in the Brahma's lifetime lasts over 4 billion human years, and is called a *kalpa*. Each of these has four yugas, four ages. The present cycle of human history began with the first yuga, which was a time of order and peace. During the second yuga, things began to fall apart and have continued to do so. We are presently in the fourth and bleakest age, when the human race's worst instincts and behaviors are on display, and it will continue this way for the next 400,000 years or so. Then things will calm down and start all over again. So begins another day in Brahma's lifetime.

Buddhists take an equally long view. "This world, most Buddhists believe, is one of the billion worlds that make up a world system. All of these billion world systems in the cosmos go through cyclical periods of production, abiding, destruction, and disappearance," writes Anne Klein in an essay about Buddhism.

Siddhartha Gautama is believed to have been born around 560 BCE in northeastern India (some scholars now place his birth around 490 BCE). He was not the first Buddha, which means "enlightened one," to appear in the world, but the others lived during prehistory, and their teachings are lost. Gautama was born into a noble Hindu family of the Shakya clan and lived in comfort and luxury with his wife, whom he married at sixteen, and their son. At the age of twenty-nine, however, he saw clearly that all beings age and die, that this is a world driven by suffering for one and all. Overwhelmed by his need to understand the human condition, he renounced family and property and set forth in the world. At thirty-five, he achieved enlightenment, while sitting under a pipal, a fig tree, and for the remaining forty-five years of his life, he taught what he had come to understand about the world and how we can disengage from its travails. "On the eve of his enlightenment, Gautama saw the cyclical birth, death and rebirth of all living things everywhere," writes Klein. "He recalled innumerable past lives, both others' and his own, linking this knowledge with a direct understanding of the process of karma, the cause and effect of actions."

Buddha's message was simple and revolutionary. Forget about the gods and forget about caste. Anyone can take on the task of worship and practice and, with hard work and single-mindedness, reach enlightenment. After Buddha's death, Buddhism developed two primary branches. The oldest was Theravada, also called Hinayana (meaning "lesser vehicle"), which was practiced in Burma, Sri Lanka, and southeast Asia. Mahayana ("greater vehicle") began around 200 BCE, and is found chiefly in Japan, China, Korea, and some parts of Vietnam. Vajrayana, considered by many to be a third branch, grew out of Mahayana in India, beginning in the fourth-century CE, and now is practiced in Tibet and Nepal. Each branch also has its subsets of various schools. Mahayana, for instance, developed the Ch'an school in China, founded by Bodhidharma in the sixth century CE, which gradually spread through Japan as Zen, where it divided into two further schools—Soto and Rinzai. All the various branches and schools of Buddhism subscribe to a belief in a hierarchy of levels of existence into which souls are reborn, as do Hindus.

Tibetan Buddhism includes a specific set of directions for the dying on how they should die, called *The Tibetan*

Book of the Dead, or *Bar-do thos-grol*, which Eva Neumaier-Dargyay translates as "Liberation from the Intermediary State by Means of Hearing This Lore." The book is usually dated to the eighth century AD, and is a description of what awaits a person in the various states between death and rebirth. It is to be studied by the living and read into the ear of the dying as a guide for the soul to those critical days following death. The book explains that the soul of the recently deceased will immediately have a chance to step off the wheel and end the chain of rebirths, but unless people achieved self-realization in the last life, they will not seize the opportunity. Instead, still in thrall to the ego and attached to the suffering world, a soul passes through various visionary states, each explicitly described in the *Bar-do thos-grol*.

Traditionally, the Tibetan Buddhists chopped up a dead body into small pieces and left it for the birds and animals on open ground, recalling the Zoroastrian's Tower of Silence. The soul would move on, and the body was done. In the twenty-first century, with a skeptical Chinese government in place, cremation is increasingly used to dispose of the dead, again following a pattern set by Zoroastrians.

"It may be argued that nobody can talk about death with authority who has not died, and since nobody apparently has ever returned from death, how can anybody know what death is or what happens after it?" wrote a German-born Tibetan Buddhist monk and scholar, Lama Govinda, in Philip Kapleau's collection, *The Wheel of Death*.

"The Tibetan will answer: 'There is not *one* person, indeed not one living being, that has not returned from death. In fact, we have all died many deaths before we came into this incarnation. And what we call birth is merely the reverse side of death, like one of the two sides of a coin, or like a door which we call "entrance" from outside and "exit" from inside a room.

"It is much more astonishing that not everybody remembers his or her previous death, and because of this lack of remembering, most persons do not believe there was a previous death. But, likewise, they do not remember their recent birth, and yet they do not doubt that they were recently born. They forget that active memory is only a small part of our normal consciousness, and that our subconscious memory registers and preserves every past impression and experience which our waking mind fails to recall.' "

While the various Buddhist doctrines have different eschatological concepts, all share a couple of basic ideas about what happens when a person dies. The first thing is that the physical and mental components of our lives separate for the first time since birth. Then, writes Eva Neumaier-Dargyay in *Life After Death in World Religions,* "The stream of phenomena that makes up the four mental categories (emotions, sensory perceptions, responses to sensory perceptions and consciousness) is driven by karma to seek an embodiment that suits its karmic makeup."

Buddhism is relatively unconcerned with rebirth and the lives to come. For many Mahayana Buddhists the important task is to worry about what comes before death, not what comes afterwards. Kapleau tells his readers that a standard response from Zen *roshis*, the great teachers, when asked about an afterlife is: "Why do you want to know what will happen to you after you die? Find out who you are now!"

Kapleau's own teacher, Hakuun Tasutani Roshi, told his student: "If we do not change, we are lifeless. We grow and age because we are alive. The evidence of our having lived is the fact that we die. We die because we are alive. Living means birth and death. Creation and destruction signify life."

Zen Buddhism's concern is finding the path to self-realization in this life—so much to do and undo in such a short span of time. Not a moment to waste, and its focus is in learning how to untie the knot now, here, this time around. While not overly worried about the lives to come, Buddhist teachers always advise students to keep death in mind and thereby to pay ceaseless attention to the task of discovering who we are now, and how we are to carry ourselves through this world. Zen monks have a tradition of "death poems" composed as they prepare to die. Here is where they reveal the "jewel at the heart of the lotus," the diamond refined by a lifetime of meditation and right living. Kapleau reproduces some lines of Master Ikkyu Sojun written around 1480 CE in anticipation of his death:

Dimly for thirty years;
Faintly for thirty years—
Dimly and faintly for sixty years:

**At my death I pass my feces and offer them
to Brahma.**

Commenting on this poem in his collection, *Japanese Death Poems*, Yoel Hoffmann has written, "The frankness of this statement is characteristic of his [Ikkyu Sojun's] style, but it ought not to be taken as profane. The image of a dying man who can no longer control his body and who defecates in his bed is no less 'sacred' than that of a believer who brings flowers as an offering to his god; all is accepted with equanimity by the Lord of the Worlds. . . ."

At a council held around 250 BCE, Theravada Buddhists from various schools established the religion's first official doctrine. Early on, Buddhists developed an elaborate schematic for the multiple heavens and hells in creation. "There are thirty-one planes of existence into which a person can be reborn after he or she dies," explained Win Myint, a retired mathematics professor at Tennessee State University in Nashville. He is a Theravada Buddhist who was born in Myanmar (the former Burma) and has lived in the southern United States for over forty years. "We believe that a person's actions in this life, their karma, is what determines how they will be reborn. It is not a thing controlled by some outside force—call it God or whatever.

"Where you are going to be reborn depends on what your deeds have been," he told me when I visited his light-filled and lovely house in the suburbs, a few blocks from where I was raised. "The basic deeds that Buddhists are taught to live by are: avoid evil, do good, purify the mind."

In 2004, Myint was invited to Barcelona's Forum on World Religions to talk about his beliefs. He was a founder of Nashville's first Buddhist temple. He moved to the city in 1965, having left Burma when he graduated from high school. He got degrees at Rensaleer Polytechnic Institute, worked as an engineer for IBM, taught for a year in Tuskeegee Institute ("out in the boondocks in Alabama"), and came to Nashville to teach at Tennessee State, a traditionally African-American university. A short man whose own skin is a rich golden brown, he has always dealt with the question of race by concentrating on the human race and paying no attention to skin color. He moves between Nashville's races, neighborhoods, and ethnic identities as easily as a fish swimming in water.

The number of Buddhists in Nashville was in the low hundreds when he arrived. In 2005, when we spoke, nearly three thousand Buddhists from all three major branches of the faith called Nashville their home. Belief in rebirth has always been a part of Myint's life, he told me. He grew up in a village outside the capital, Mandelay, now called Rangoon, or Yangon. "In my case, one of my playmates had a younger brother who always liked to go visit a lady who lived not far from his house. He was the rebirth of her husband. He always wanted to be around her. When he was grown up, he took the woman, who by then was an old lady, and led her to a corner of the yard of her house, and asked for permission to dig at that spot. He dug, and there was a sack of gold hidden that he had forgotten to tell his wife was there before he died. I didn't see it, but a lot of people did and told me about it. That's proof for me.

"In Western culture, children are discouraged from talking about these kinds of memories. They are ashamed to talk about it, but we need to encourage them to talk about it, because it may help them toward enlightenment."

What constitutes "proof" for Win Myint is not enough for a lot of people. One Westerner who has attempted to validate children's claims of reincarnation using the tools of social science is Ian Stevenson. He served until his retirement as a chaired professor of psychiatry at the University of Virginia's medical school and dedicated himself to investigating past-life recall. In the 1960s, he began investigating and analyzing reports of people who remembered their past lives. Eventually he had gathered data from over two thousand cases, mostly from southeast Asia but also including examples from the Middle East, Europe, the United States, and Latin America. He spent long periods of time interviewing people about their memories of other lives, then investigating the details of their stories. He also did extensive research on people born with birthmarks and birth defects who claimed they were the marks and effects of violence done to them in previous lives.

If a child claimed to have lived in another village during his or her last life and provided details of that life, Stevenson journeyed to the place to try to determine if indeed such a person had lived and died there. He found many details that matched exactly, uncannily, and over the years he became absolutely convinced that he was witnessing genuine instances of reincarnation.

Stevenson's multiple volumes make for hard going. He tries to organize his material in an analytical, objective fashion, which often does little more than make it difficult to read. A book by Tom Shroder called *Old Souls: The Scientific Evidence for Past Lives* is a generally sympathetic journalistic account of Stevenson and his work, by an author who is a *Washington Post* staff member and who was allowed to accompany the reincarnationist on his field trips. The tale told is impressive, as case history after case history unfolds on Stevenson's visits to Hindus in India and Druse in Lebanon in which there seems to be no other acceptable explanation than reincarnation for how a child in one place might accurately "remember" correct details from a past life in another.

Shroder, an editor and journalist by trade, does try to provide readers with a bit of balance for his own positive assessment of Stevenson's work. He quotes a "former associate" of the researcher who criticizes Stevenson for asking leading questions, conducting superficial investigations, not taking into sufficient account the "human fallibility" of the witnesses he interviews, and reporting the cases in a way that makes them sound more impressive than they actually are. Overall, however, Shroder finds the evidence compelling.

Not everyone is persuaded by Stevenson's science. Paul

Edwards, a philosophy professor at the New School in New York City, and an indefatigable critic of reincarnation theory in each and all of its forms wrote a book called *Reincarnation: A Critical Examination,* published by any debunking specialist's favorite publisher, Prometheus Books. Stevenson's work came in for particularly sharp criticism. His cases read much more convincingly in summary than when read closely, Edwards concluded, adding that he found substantial gaps in those he examined, and he enumerates them. However, the details are just icing on the cake, he writes, because the entire premise underlying Stevenson's work is spurious. "Even in the absence of a demonstration of specific flaws, a rational person will conclude either that Stevenson's reports are seriously defective or that his alleged facts can be explained without bringing in reincarnation."

Whether or not they are convinced by Stevenson's research, most observers would agree that his is an honest effort at scientific investigation of reincarnation, perhaps the first in history. While his work convinced him that reincarnation does exist, he was unable to draw any conclusions about the process itself, or the how and the why of it. Even in India, where Stevenson found the majority of his cases, those who claimed to recall a past life were relatively rare, and most people, although they believed in reincarnation, did not have any memories about other lives. In an interview with Tom Shroder, Stevenson speculated: "Maybe remembering [a past life] is a defect. Maybe we're supposed to forget, but sometimes that system malfunctions, and we don't forget completely."

A belief in reincarnation has been present in major branches of Western culture going all the way back to at least ancient Greece. Not all Greeks embraced the possibility of reincarnation, but among those who did were some of Greece's most influential minds. "Once on a time a youth was I, and I was a maiden, a bush, a bird, and a fish with scales that gleam in the ocean," wrote Empedocles in the fifth century BCE.

A hundred years before Empedocles, the Greek mathematician and scientist Pythagoras, who was the first Westerner to say the earth was round, was also the first to go on record affirming reincarnation. Well, not exactly on record, because there are no extant writings by Pythagoras that deal with reincarnation, but from those who followed him, like Empedocles, we know that Pythagoras proclaimed a doctrine of rebirth. Scholars do not doubt that he believed in universal reincarnation and established a brotherhood to study it, according to John Sanford in *Soul Journey: A Jungian Analyst Looks at Reincarnation*. In fact, reported Empedocles, Pythagoras had described numerous of his past lives, which he remembered clearly.

Plato wrote about reincarnation in the fifth century BCE. "Let us consider [life after death] by asking whether the souls of men who have died are in the nether world or not," he wrote in the *Phaedo*. "There is an ancient tradition, which we remember, that they go from here and come back here again and are born from the dead."

The Celts also were reported by none other than Julius Caesar to have had a well-defined belief in reincarnation. In his *Gallic Wars*, he wrote that they believed "souls do not become extinct but pass after death from one body to another and they think that men by this tenet are in a greater degree incited to valour, the fear of death being disregarded."

The Jews were also developing a theory of reincarnation that continued over millennia as a stream feeding into the river of Jewish eschatology. It is a current that has been directed underground, out of sight, since the late Middle Ages, when Jews attempted more and more to integrate themselves into the Christian world around them, to blend in, to become like chameleons in adapting to their surroundings in response to the violent anti-Semitism threatening them in virtually every generation. While not openly discussed, the idea that the dead will be reincarnated has always been present in a segment of Jewish thought.

In his book *Reincarnation and Judaism: The Journey of the Soul*, DovBer Pinson writes: "When speaking of reincarnation, the soul we speak of is the Godly soul. It is this soul which reincarnates. . . . This is the soul that is 'Truly, a part of the God above.' It is self-evident that the soul is infinite and everlasting and ultimately immortal. It existed before the creation of the body and will exist well after the body disintegrates."

Kabbalistic teachings about reincarnation were not generally available to Jewish believers and were transmitted

secretly for over a thousand years. At first they were communicated orally between generations and then by means of
notes. The first kabbalistic books mentioning reincarnation,
according to Pinson, are the *Bahir* and the *Zohar*, dating
back to the last part of the thirteenth century. Catalonia—
the southwest of France and northeast of Spain—was a
cradle of kabbalistic exposition. A large body of writings was
generated by the great kabbalistic rabbis of the Middle
Ages, and the soul's fate after death was discussed with as
much certainty as it is today in central Tennessee. It was the
last era of peace that European Jewry would have for six
centuries. The descendants of the great kabbalistic rabbis
were uprooted and driven from pillar to post around
Europe, murdered and deported. Kabbalistic doctrine
reverted to a dedicated, discreet few.

Early Christianity also had an esoteric belief system incorporating reincarnation. Not Roman Catholics, nor Protestants, nor any other mainline Christian denomination
accepts the possibility of reincarnation, but since its beginnings the Church has harbored schools of esoteric thought,
and some of these have found reincarnation not incompatible with Jesus Christ's message. The Gnostics believed in
reincarnation for a small part of the population—those who
carried within them some small part of the divinity and who
were journeying through life after life until reunified with
the divine.

For instance, in Carl Schmidt's edition of the *Pistis
Sophia*, a Gnostic work written in Coptic, in book 3, chapter

125, Mary Magdalene questions Jesus after his Resurrection. " 'My Lord, if the faith and the mysteries have come to be revealed, now at this time when souls come into the world in many cycles and they neglect to receive mysteries, being confident that when they come into the world to other cycles they will receive them, are they not therefore in danger that they do not attain to receiving the mysteries?'

"The Saviour answered and said to his disciples: 'Preach to the whole world and say to men: strive that you receive the mysteries of the light in this restricted time, so that you go into the Kingdom of the Light. Do not spend day upon day or cycle upon cycle being confident that you will attain to receiving the mysteries when you come into the world in another cycle. And these do not know when the time of the perfect souls will come about, for when the number of perfect souls exists I will shut the gates of the light. And no one will go within from this hour.' "

Carpocratians were members of a branch of Gnosticism, who named themselves after Carpocrates, generally thought to have lived in the second century CE. They believed that all people's souls were reincarnated through the entire variation of human existences until rejoining the divine. Countless lifetimes dedicated to good and countless others to evil, experiencing in flesh and blood the world and all its human variations until, after vast a time, the souls are reunited with that from which they sprang. Another of its tenets was reputedly complete sexual freedom for male believers, who were free to interchange wives at will, and the Carpocratians were roundly decried for their licentiousness. Their critics agreed that it was virtually a pagan faith, making the barest use of Christian rites and doctrine.

Buddhists and Hindus share the Carpocratian conviction that we will pass through countless lifetimes, experiencing all the multiple forms life assumes. But they do not find in this belief a basis for excess. Buddhists, in particular, believe that living many lives provides a basis for compassion, which is the Buddhist key to living in the world and which imposes a responsibility on each human. We are all in this same boat together, all suffering the cycle of birth and death, dying endlessly, each one of us. This should call forth compassion toward every sentient being.

"From the belief in beginningless reincarnation it follows that we have been in every possible relationship with everyone else," writes Ann Klein. "Most significantly, everyone has been a great friend and even our own mother at some time in the past; hence it is appropriate to have compassion and concern for them, no matter what their present situation is or how they now behave toward us."

Compassion does not seem to have been a key tenet of Carpocrates's thinking from the little we know about him. Irenaeus lived at approximately the same time as Carpocrates. He wrote against a belief in reincarnation, and it is from him and others who refuted Carpocrates and the Gnostics in general that we have an idea of what the Carpocratians represented. Carpocrates himself left no written record, or if he did, it has long since been destroyed. His ecclesiastical enemies, however, do not hesitate to fully describe and decry his heresies.

Carpocrates had a son named Epiphanes who died at the tender age of seventeen. Young as he was, he nonetheless penned a letter concerning justice and righteousness, which was reproduced by a number of those who railed against his father. It reads in part: "For man God made all things to be common property. He brought the female to be with the male in common and in the same way united all animals. He thus showed righteousness to be a universal sharing along with equality. But those who have been born in this way have denied the sharing which is the corollary of their origin and say Let him who has taken one woman keep her, whereas all can share her, just as the animals show us. With view to the permanence of the race he has implanted in males a strong and ardent desire which neither law nor custom nor any other restraint is able to destroy."

Both material goods and women were to be shared in the ideal world envisioned by Carpocrates. "So unbridled is their madness, that they declare they have in their power all things which are irreligious and impious, and they are at liberty to practice them," wrote Irenaeus of Lyons in the second century. "They deem it necessary, therefore, that by means of transmigration from body to body, souls should have experience of every kind . . . in order that, as their writings express it, their souls, having made trial of every kind of life, may, at their departure, not be wanting in any particular."

In a Web site created by Anthony Subias, Carpocrates is cited as the founding father of a line of thought that leads through the Marquis de Sade in the eighteenth century, living out cruelty in all its possible forms, to Aleister Crowley in the twentieth century saying, "Do what thou will shall be the whole of the law." Viewed as such, Carpocrates's teaching is entering its second millennium. It has, however, been a highly discreet survival, always at the margins of organized religion. By the sixth century, reincarnation had virtually disappeared from Christian dialogue; no one was writing against it because it was no longer an issue.

This does not mean that a belief in reincarnation disappeared entirely from the world, but it went underground, nourished in the more esoteric teachings of the montheisms— the Kabbalah for the Jews, Gnosticism for the Christians, underground streams of knowledge that have survived down through the centuries. Islam, too, has contributed to this body of hidden knowledge, tradition, ritual, and rite, affirming a belief in rebirth. The Druse are members of a surviving religion that grew out of Islam who believe in reincarnation by all human souls into new human bodies. The religion was founded in the ninth century by Muslims who separated from the mainstream faith; faced with persecution by the Islamic majority, the Druse disguised their worship and practiced their faith in secret. Some of the cases of children recalling past lives that Ian Stevenson believes point most convincingly toward reincarnation are in Druse communities.

An estimated one million Druse, or Druze, as it is alternatively written, practice the religion in the world today, and not much has been learned over the past thousand years about what their beliefs are and how they worship. They call themselves the Mowahhidoon and are an independent, staunchly monotheistic people. Some 600,000 of them are thought to be living in the Middle East in Lebanon, Syria, and Israel, where they are the only Arab Israelis who serve in the Israeli army. Some Druse do not think of themselves as Arabs, while others have a strong identification with the Palestinian cause and are staunchly anti-Israel. In addition to the Druse in the Middle East, another 300,000 or so live around the world in places as far-flung as North America, Australia, Latin America, and Europe.

It is known that Druse society is essentially divided into two categories: the great bulk of believers, who live their daily lives in faith but without access to the sacred books and teachings, and a minority of adepts, who transmit the esoteric knowledge. The Qur'an is considered a sacred book, but it is viewed as a receptacle for a hidden knowledge not evident to all. All Druse believe they will be reborn through a long series of successive bodies until they are reunited with the divine from which all creation arose.

The mainstream monotheisms entirely reject any concept of a soul reborn in a new body. Most Jews are entirely ignorant of any tradition of transmigration in the faith's history. Muslims energetically renounce the possibility, pointing to the clear explanation in Islam of what happens to us when we die. Not a single mainstream Christian Church incorporates even a whiff of a reincarnation doctrine. All of them absolutely refute the idea of a soul reborn in a different body. So it is particularly surprising in a fundamentalist nation like the United States that a lot of professed Christians are willing to admit the possibility of reincarnation. In fact, a 1994 Gallup poll found that 27 percent of people in the United States believed in reincarnation, and another 20 percent were not sure, leaving only a bare majority willing to say reincarnation does not exist. Well, who can blame them? Most people would prefer not to die—would prefer to continue living forever in full vigor, enjoying all life's nuanced pleasures. But if a body has to crumble, then at least to live on in spirit, in soul, is better than not living on at all. It is better than nothing, which appears to be the other alternative, and it is not surprising that people are reluctant to rule it out entirely.

Rebirth is not the only means by which people believe a soul might survive. The Roman Catholic Church, with some 900 million members around the world, has its own doctrine of the soul's journey after death. What is the entity called a soul? The Church's catechism defines it as "a living being without a body, having reason and free will." The soul separates from the dead body immediately after a person dies, and it undergoes the first of two judgments. These are called the Particular and the General judgments. The soul will spend the rest of the life of the world in heaven, hell, or purgatory, depending on the outcome of the Particular Judgment. Then time will end, and a final General Judgment for all eternity will be held for every resurrected body rejoined with every soul.

The Particular Judgment means that no sooner do we draw our last breaths than we know whether heaven and closeness to God are our immediate lot, there to wait for the final and General Judgment. Christian mystics, according to John Hick in *Death and Eternal Life*, traditionally explained, "Throw a bar of iron into a blazing furnace and leave it there till it is molten metal in the midst of the fire and the eye can no longer see the iron. As that iron knows the fire, so shall we know God. Our inmost being will thrill and throb in unison with God's life and we shall be fully conscious of it."

If we die in a state of sanctifying grace, that is, baptized and with no unabsolved mortal sins on our souls but with some unabsolved venial ones, our souls go to purgatory to serve out a purification process that will cleanse us of the sins we carried with us when we died and prepare us to experience God's direct, divine love. Purgatory is an indefinite period of time that will be necessary to prepare a soul to experience the divine. The process of cleansing souls in purgatory is also advanced by the intercessory prayers of our families on earth.

"Catholic teaching insists on the reality of Purgatory, a condition (rather than a place) of transition and adaptation for those entering heavenly beatitude," writes Roman

Catholic theologian Francis Cleary. "Even great saints know sin during earthly life and die affected by selfish self-centeredness incompatible with divine intimacy. Purgatory describes the passage, at once painful and joyful, into purified existence. Then only can persons accept and return God's overwhelming love without hindrance."

However, the life of the soul is not an eternal one. The soul is being prepared to rejoin the body at the end of time, following an immeasurable period in which the soul will have its own existence. The second judgment that awaits all human beings is the General, when Jesus the Christ returns and the judgment is at hand that will send all souls to their eternal destinies. It is hard enough to pass through the first, the Particular Judgment, our own end, the weighing of all our deeds, every time we bowed our knees before the easier choice, all our petty sins and our grave ones. Have we done even a feather's weight of good in the world, a question asked three thousand years ago by the Egyptians and expressed with the feather *maat*, and still awaiting each of us at the Particular Judgment? Beyond that, who can even begin to imagine the terrible beauty of the General Judgment, when the world as we have known it has ended and a final irrevocable judgment is handed down on one and all.

For those who are neither in a state of grace nor saved by a confession of belief in Jesus Christ the Redeemer, hell's yawning maws are waiting. Pope John Paul II described hell as a condition of pain that results from alienation from God, a condition that one brings on oneself. However, this should not be interpreted to mean that hell has no physical reality, that we shall not have to suffer fire and brimstone in the flesh, according to Josep Maria Martí Bonet, a canon who is the Barcelona Diocese's official historian and director of its archives and the diocesan museum.

The unsaved, those whom God passes over, are sentenced to eternal damnation, and they will feel it in the flesh forever, he said. "The worst punishment is to be separated from God through what we have brought on ourselves, and hell is, undoubtedly, a state of separation from God. However, Jesus Christ himself spoke numerous times of the fire, and it has to mean something. Our doctrine holds that hell is no doubt a state, but it also has to be something physical, particularly because we're speaking here of the resurrection of the flesh for all times."

The building in which Martí Bonet has his office and where the archives are housed is located on Bishop's Street, a narrow medieval street that leads from the cathedral and the diocesan offices to the Plaça Sant Jaume, the square where both the city hall and the Catalan government's offices are located. Bishop Street literally joins church and state, with one at either end. From Martí Bonet's office in the Diocese's administrative complex in a fourteenth-century palace, the view is across a line of exuberant palm trees to the cathedral, and its deep bell tolled to interrupt our interview each quarter hour. We sat facing each other on wide, high-backed ecclesiastical chairs with broad wooden arms and red plush-velvet cushions beneath and behind the sitter.

The church has been an inextricable part of Catalonia and Barcelona since at least 64 CE, he said, when the first documentary mention is found of the cities of Tarraco—present-day Tarragona—and Barcino—Barcelona—outposts of the Roman Empire on the Mediterranean shores of the Iberian peninsula. By the beginning of the fourth century, Barcelona had produced martyrs who were later beatified, figures like Saint Cugat and Saint Eulalia. As the Roman Empire's influence dwindled, the Roman Church's influence grew, the one God eclipsed the many, and Christians were no longer underdogs. Since the Middle Ages, the Church has been a major player in the history of Catalonia.

Things have not really changed. Although attendance at Mass in Spanish churches has plummeted over the past thirty years, and the Church no longer dictates state policy as it did in the decades of Francisco Franco's dictatorship, the influence of Spanish clergy in the Vatican increased significantly under the long pontificate of John Paul II. The shadowy and ultraconservative Spanish Catholic society Opus Dei enjoyed ever greater access to the pope, its founder was canonized and its members installed in high places. When a canon of the Catalan Church addresses himself to doctrine, he generally does so with certainty.

"I'm absolutely convinced that we'll enjoy eternity in our bodies and we'll be able to recognize each other and our families will be together again," Martí Bonet told me, as the voices of children playing somewhere nearby drifted in the open office windows on the hot summer morning air. No air conditioning in this stone palace.

He spoke slowly, softly, with absolute conviction. "We'll be able to speak with people whose lives are important to us, someone whose writings we've studied, whose thoughts we've read and admired, we'll speak to them and they'll speak to us. Immortality—it's the fundamental question. Do you believe or not? That's it—that's the most important thing."

Between our individual deaths and the General Judgment, our souls live out the Particular Judgment, while the body "rests" in the grave awaiting the final hour. At that time, Roman Catholic doctrine joins that of the Protestant Churches to describe an eternity spent in one's old form. How exactly that will happen is imaginable only for God, but that it will happen is a given, accepted absolutely. We shall not occupy quite the same body but a new, improved version of the old one we left in the grave.

"At the end of the world, the flesh will be resurrected, and certainly it will be in the maximum of youth and plenitude and we shall be more handsome than we ever were in this life," said Martí Bonet, nodding his head slowly in contemplation and awe of the delights to come. "The resurrection of the flesh will be a work of God, and as such, it will be free from defects. At the beginning of the Church, people had trouble understanding the resurrection awaiting everyone, because they knew that the body corrupted and decomposed. Saint Paul himself said that from a mere seed, from virtually the shadow of a person, God could make that body, that flesh live again."

It calls to mind the Jewish concept of the Luz, the tiniest bit of bone necessary to reconstruct an entire human being. It also calls to mind stem cells, those tiny repositories of our entire individual genome. For Martí Bonet, what it calls to mind is immortality: "This is what we proclaim and repeat in our Creed; it is absolutely fundamental to us that we believe in the resurrection of the flesh and in life everlasting."

For Roman Catholics and many other monotheists as well, the soul's eternal destiny is a physical body in Paradise. For most Asian religions, the longed-for destiny of the soul is a dissolution back into the original essence from which it arose. This is as true for Taoists in China as it is for Hindus and Buddhists, although Taoist believers focus less attention on eschatology than do Buddhists or Hindus. Nevertheless, a pattern is plain throughout the world's religions. The earliest prophets and scribes, the founders of the great faiths, all devote the great bulk of their instruction to propounding how we must live now, confronted with this world and its daily temptations and suffering, and they spend little or no time considering what is to come after death. As the seeds of these faiths take root and sprout, however, those who follow the founders spend an increasing amount of time and energy on describing the world to come and what we can expect to happen after we die.

At more or less the same moment in history, around the fifth century BCE, give or take a century, Sakyamuni Buddha was alive in India, Plato was pursuing philosophy in Athens, Ezekiel was writing from exile in Babylon, and China's two great currents of religious thought, Confucianism and Taoism, were born. Ancient oral teachings about the Tao ("the way") were being collected and written down in the *Tao Te Ching*, and Confucius is believed to have lived from 572 to 479 BCE.

Of all the world's major religions, the most focused on the here-and-now and paying the least concern to an afterlife is Confucianism, even more so than Judaism. In fact, some scholars argue that it is not a religion at all, because in addition to lacking a clear eschatology, it has no ecclesiastical infrastructure. "It has no priesthood, no church, no bible, no creed, no conversion, and no fixed system of gods," writes Vergilius Ferm in *An Encyclopedia of Religion*.

Nevertheless, Confucius elaborated his morally and politically ordered ideal society on a ground in which the afterlife was a broad substrate. The Chinese practiced an ancient religion based on reverence for ancestors in a universe with two principal forces of energy at play in the creation and unfolding of the world: yin and yang. Family, the blood bond, was the means of coming into being and our path to immortality. The individual, however, lived and died but once. S. G. F. Brandon explains it in his book, *The Judgment of the Dead*.

"The primitive Chinese believed that the family stock

[*la substance familiale*] was everlasting and counterterminous with the earth upon which the family had its habitation and from the products of which its members lived. This *substance familiale* lay buried beneath the ground as *une masse indistincte*, and it was represented above ground, at any given moment, only by the living members of the family, which constituted, as it were, the individualized portion of the family stock. It followed, accordingly, that each birth within the family represented the reincarnation of a portion of the subterranean *substance familiale*, while each death meant in effect the return of a part of the individualized family stock to the *masse indistincte* in the ground below."

Confucius never seems to have explicitly refuted this idea. His concern was for ordering life in the present and living it in such a way as to benefit oneself and the community of which each person formed a part. In one of Confucius's Analects, a disciple named Jilu asked about the service of ghosts and spirits. Confucius replied, "You have never been able to serve people. On what basis would you serve ghosts?"

With the temerity of the uninitiated, Jilu went on: "I venture to ask about death."

"You have never understood life," Confucius answers. "On what basis would you understand death?"

Even after Confucianism began to be widely practiced, the old beliefs survived, and a certain syncretism took place. By the fourth century BCE, people subscribed to the idea that each individual has two souls, a yin soul affiliated with the earth that is of the body, created at the moment of conception, and called *kuei* after death; and a soul that is of heavenly origin, associated with air and breath, which enters a body at the moment a baby draws its first breath to make its first cry, and is called *shen* after death.

Brandon quotes a passage from the *Li Chi*, composed between 200 BCE and 200 CE, which claimed to be a record of Confucius's teachings.

"Tsai Wo said, 'I have heard the names of kuei and shen, but I do not know what they mean.' The Master said, "All creatures inevitably come to die. Dying they inevitably go back to earth. This is what is meant by kuei. The bones and the flesh molder below, and, hidden there, make the soil of the land. But the breath soars aloft to become light, and is found in the fragrance and the feeling of sorrow at the sacrifice.""

"The feeling of sorrow at the sacrifice"—what a striking phrase. This is how one best describes the rising soul, the bit of divine essence in each of us. The sacrifice of our own lives after an all-too-brief span, during which we sacrifice other lives to maintain our own. The fragrance of life, its evanescent sweetness and pleasures. Ours is not to worry about what comes after death, but to live our lives correctly in this world. The main contribution of Confucianism was the order it brought into daily life, insisting that human society should reflect heavenly society, that our lives should be as well organized, as merciful, as implacable, as moral, and as correct as heaven. Its message was one of order in the political, social, and economic spheres as well as in the individual lives of its followers. As it spread across East Asia it influenced and was influenced by local beliefs. The locus for its message was in this world, in the lives of individuals, the states they formed, the rulers who ordered them, not only in China, but also in Korea and Japan, where Confucianism spread and took root. Buddhist beliefs about the afterlife were absorbed in much the same way as ancestor worship or a devotion to Taoism and all of these were embraced and woven together into a lively, living religion with little difficulty.

Aligning one's life and community with the principles that order the world and heaven is no easy task. Effort and study are required. For instance, one of the most important books in Confucian literature is the *Yi Jing*, which we know as the *I Ching* or *The Book of Changes*. It is one of the purest components of Confucianism to have crossed from East to West during the twentieth century, with the translation by Richard Wilhelm originally published in English in 1967 and still selling briskly in 2006. It consists of sixty-four different hexagrams, and each of these contains a brief instruction, or parable, or homily. The *Yi Jing* is used as a book of divination by throwing out yarrow sticks and gathering them into hexagrams, which are then consulted. To do so properly requires study and attention.

Taoism, China's other great homegrown religion, also took formal shape around the beginning of the fifth century BCE, incorporating many Confucian tenets. In fact, Taoist tradition has it that Lao-zi and Confucius met on several occasions and had dialogues (in which Lao-zi consistently came out better than Confucius). His name is rendered in our alphabet by a number of different spellings, Lao-zi, or Laotse, Lao-tzu or Lao-zu, all of which are translated as "old master." He is credited with authorship of the *Tao Te Ching* (*The Way and Its Power*), the first book about the Tao and the first collected instructions for those who wished to follow it.

People who mastered the teachings would enjoy longevity in this life and immortality in the next. The afterlife was almost beside the point for the early Taoists, however, because their practice was for the purpose of understanding this life at hand, to live correctly in total awareness. Only scant attention was paid to what happens after death, until the incursion of Buddhism into China and its gradual incorporation into Taoist thought, a process that began around the first century CE. Then, gradually, the idea of karma, of levels of existence, of heavens and hells began to assume a prominence in Taoist thought, and immortality became the just deserts of those who lived the Tao in this life.

In parallel with the European world, alchemy was developed among the Taoists apparently wholly independently of the West, beginning with the Song Dynasty, founded in 960 CE. The road to longevity in this life and immortality afterwards could be achieved by combining physical changes induced by the ingestion of certain elements such as jade, gold, and mercury with meditation designed to use the elements of our mental lives to create a different mind and approach to life.

For those who wished to follow the Tao to realization and immortality, alchemy in both its forms—operative and inner—was invaluable. By the twelfth century, it began to emerge as an important part of the school of Complete Perfection, which became one of Taoism's most important branches and is one that endures today. An elaborate regimen of infusions, powders, elixirs, and pills was followed, as well as a meditative practice that was the mental equivalent of the physical treatments.

"In meditation as in the process of operative alchemy, these energies are revolved again and again, following an exact time schedule and being properly positioned according to the traditional stems and branches of the calendar and the compass," according to Livia Kohn in *The Taoist Experience*. "The cycle that is established within the body at this point includes not only the spine and the breastbone, but also leads through the five orbs. It is known as the macrocosmic orbit.

"At this stage the pure power of yin and yang is extracted from the various energies, and symbolized in the trigrams of Heaven and Earth (Qian and Kun). These are at the root of creation, to which the adept is gradually proceeding.

"In the third and last stage, the immortal embryo, still semi-material, is transformed into the pure spirit body of the immortals. . . . The child is born, completed and begins an independent existence. It can ascend to the heavens and will be in the form in which the practitioner survives forever."

In addition to the importance placed on inner and operative alchemical practices, other profound changes took place in Taoism under the Song Dynasty that would remain as part of its doctrine. These developments were connected to the process of integrating Taoism, Confucianism, and Buddhism, and what eventually emerged was a large religious tent under which practitioners of many stripes could feel comfortable.

While distinct from one another in many ways, the religions of Asia generally do not espouse the resurrection of the physical body but do hold that our souls live on after our deaths. These are ancient faiths held by vast numbers of people. Together they form an impressive cosmology, a profound attempt to explain the unknowable universe. They have served billions of people as their polestars, something by which they could orient their daily lives and invest them with meaning.

Despite the obvious gulf between the eschatologies of East and West, scholars and believers alike have found that Asian religion is by no means wholly separate from or irreconcilable with the monotheisms of the West. The Cistercian monk Thomas Merton found many similarities between monastic life in the Abbey of Gethsemani in Kentucky, where he lived, and the lives of monks in Asia. In his book, *Zen and the Birds of Appetite*, he included an essay by D. T. Suzuki, "Wisdom in Emptiness." Suzuki was a Japanese scholar and Zen Buddhist whose books about Zen were among the first written in lucid English. In the essay, Suzuki equates the Zen notion of emptiness with the Christian notion of poverty. He quotes the song of Kyogen Chikan, a Zen master from 800 CE:

> **Last year's poverty was not yet perfect;**
> **This year's poverty is absolute.**
> **In last year's poverty there was room for the head of a**
> **   gimlet;**
> **This year's poverty has let the gimlet itself disappear.**

Then he quotes Meister Eckhardt, the thirteenth-century German mystic, writing about the saints. "Saint Peter said, 'We have left all things.' Saint James said, 'We have given up all things.' Saint John said, 'We have nothing left.' Whereupon Brother Eckhardt asks, 'When do we leave all things? When we leave everything conceivable, everything expressible, everything audible, everything visible, then and then only we give up all things. When in this sense we give up all, we grow aflood with light, passing bright with God.' "

Suzuki continues, "Kyogen the Zen Master says: 'This year's poverty has let the gimlet itself disappear.' This is symbolical. In point of fact it means that one is dead to oneself, corresponding to:

> *Visankharagatam cittam,*
> **Gone to dissolution is the mind,**

Tanhanam khayam ajjhaga.
The cravings have come to an end.

"This is part of the verse ascribed to Buddha when he attained the supreme enlightenment, and it is known as the 'Hymn of Victory.' The gimlet is 'dissolved,' the body is 'dissolved,' the mind is 'dissolved,' all is 'dissolved'—is this not Emptiness? In other words, it is the perfect state of poverty."

In an essay called "The Significance of the Bhagavad-Gita," written shortly before he died in 1968, Merton stressed the common ground shared by those who sought spiritual truth, be they Taoists, Hindus, Buddhists, or Christians.

It is in surrendering a false and illusory liberty on the superficial level that man unites himself with the inner ground of reality and freedom in himself which is the will of God, of Krishna, of Providence, of Tao. These concepts do not all exactly coincide, but they have much in common. It is by remaining open to an infinite number of unexpected possibilities which transcend his own imagination and capacity to plan that man really fulfills his own need for freedom. The *Gita*, like the Gospels, teaches us to live in awareness of an inner truth that exceeds the grasp of our thought and cannot be subject to our own control. In following mere appetite for power we are slaves of appetite. In obedience to that truth we are at last free.

In addition to a mutually searching spirit among those who devote their lives to seeking the truth, some scholars have pointed to a concept of the human mind that is shared between scientists and those who practice meditation on a deep level. The task in deep meditation is to reach the basic cellular level shared by all beings, to know human nature, and thereby to understand one's own nature. The goal is to reach an awareness at a cellular level, a neuronal knowledge. This kind of practice was typified by Tenzin Palmo, born in London in 1943 and raised there, who left England at the age of twenty for India to study Tibetan Buddhism. She became the first fully ordained Tibetan Buddhist nun from the West and spent a dozen years living in a cave in the Himalayan mountains in India, three of those years under a vow of silence, with most of each day spent in meditation. "I was never bored," was her commentary on the experience.

In a book by Vicki Mackenzie about Tenzin Palmo's life, *Cave in the Snow*, Robert Thurman, a professor of Indo-Tibetan studies at Columbia University and a writer of big-selling books about Buddhism, is quoted as equating this sort of deep meditation with scientific investigation into the most basic components of brain function. "What the meditator is doing in those long retreats is a very technical thing," according to Thurman. "He's not just sitting there communicating with the great oneness. He's technically going down and pulling apart his own nervous system to become self-aware from out of his own cells. In other words, the Mahayana Buddhist, filled with technical understanding of

tantra, has become a quantum physicist of inner reality. . . .
He's gone down to the most subtle neuronal level or supra-
neuronal level. The yogi goes right down to below machine
language—below the sub-atomic level."

Thurman continues by insisting that he is not describing
"a mystical thing but some very concrete evolutionary
thing. It's the highest level of evolution. That's what the
Buddha is defined as: the highest level of evolution."

The twentieth century was the first in which Buddhism
was widely practiced in the West. By the twenty-first century, all the major schools of Buddhism had established
themselves in the United States and Europe. Buddhism is
now an everyday reality for many Westerners. Most of them
believe in the rebirth of the soul, as do many of those who
are yoga practitioners, acupuncture patients, Tai Chi adepts,
or followers of many of the other beliefs and practices that
have come to the West from the East.

Adherence to an Asian religious or cultural practice is not
required for belief in reincarnation. Polls in the United States
consistently affirm that about a quarter of the people believe
in reincarnation and another quarter are not sure about it.
These Americans are by no means all Buddhists or Yoga
practitioners. Some are, no doubt, practicing Christians and
Jews, others are New Agers, and still others follow a more
personal faith. For all of them, rebirth seems more possible
than resurrection. Many people are drawn to the idea that
some energy inside each of us does not disappear at death
but moves on—that we are reborn and die many times.

Untitled, by Patrick Regis, oil on fiberboard. Author's collection. Three Haitian women calling on spirits.

The Other Side

A monk asked a Zen Buddhist master, "What happens
when we die?

"I don't know," the master replied.

"How can you not know?" asked the student. "You're a
master."

"Yes, but I'm not a dead master."

Quoted in *Still Here* by Ram Dass

I n room 21 at a Connecticut nursing home where she has
come to die, my mother is in deep narco-sleep, with her
mouth open, jaw slack, head against the pillow, her fine gray

hair clean and brushed back by a nurse—they use some kind of dry shampoo. The clear plastic oxygen tubes in her nose lead to the machine at her bedside that helps her breathe and emits a low, rhythmic susuration. My mother's chest rises, falls, and after a long pause, rises and falls again. Burdened with a frail, weakening body, and faced with the prospect of spending whatever time remains to her bedridden, she has decided to stop taking nourishment and medication, except for pain pills. After two weeks she has slipped into a virtually round-the-clock sleep, except when she rouses to ask for more meds or something to drink. Her Oxycontin has kicked in now, and she is sleeping deeply. A woman named Susan Judge passes by the open door, looks in and smiles broadly, waving cheerily at me where I sit in an easy chair at the foot of the bed, watching my mother breathe. Judge is the center's "therapeutic recreation director." It seems like an odd job description for this place. Not everyone here is as close to death as my mother, but those who are not do not have far to go to get there.

A tall, willowy woman with pale skin, long brown hair, blue eyes, and thin, elegant fingers, part of Susan Judge's job is to animate and engage the patients. She looks younger than her fifty-five years and laughs delightedly when recounting the life that has brought her here. She had hoped to make it big in the entertainment business when she was younger, she told me, and although it hadn't worked out that way, she loves to perform and to "lift peoples' spirits." She has sing-alongs in the lounge, determinedly ignoring the fact that two of the three patients present have dozed off in their wheelchairs. I have asked her not to come into my mother's room when I am there, as she did the first few days after we arrived. Her insistent, aggressive cheeriness put me off. The time I have remaining to sit quietly and watch my mother breathe is short. Very short.

Susan Judge was raised in Connecticut as a Roman Catholic, but she "always had a desire to know more," she told me one afternoon in her office. As a young woman, she had a near-death experience. It completely changed her life. She is absolutely certain about what happens to us when we die, because God effectively granted her knowledge of the afterlife. "I was pregnant with my second child when I was twenty-six years old. It was a difficult delivery and I lost lots of blood. At one point I realized I was going to die.

"I spoke with God and asked to say farewell to my family. Within an hour, almost all of them had come to my bedside. As they stood there, I was drawn out of my body and was looking down from the ceiling at them. I could hear them speaking to me and could hear the thoughts in their minds. Their words didn't match their thoughts. For instance, my sister was congratulating me on the birth, but I could hear her thinking, 'She looks awful.' I was frustrated they didn't acknowledge the fact I was trying to say goodbye. For some reason I came back into my body. I felt weight again. I didn't feel well and didn't want to be there.

"Later that evening, I had my hands on the bed rails and felt something vibrating and heard a noise like a vacuum cleaner. I was vibrating, not the bed rails. I heard a loud clap and I was totally out of my body, floating on the ceiling. It was black. I felt terrible grief and loneliness. I moved toward a gray area; there was a circle, and in the center was a pinhole of white light. I tried to make my way there, it was like swimming down what seemed to be a tunnel.

"I went to the light and it was a person—the absolute form of love and intelligence. Greater than myself. This warmth of love was the most I ever experienced. This person knew who I was. It was a very humbling experience. I had an entire life's review and communicated to this being that's all I had to offer and I realized it wasn't very much, that I was not worthy, and that it would be okay if he eliminated that presence."

Her eyes filled with tears remembering it, nearly thirty years later behind her desk in a Connecticut nursing home. "This being said to me, 'That's all I ask, that you give me what you have and I accept you as you are and I now wipe you clean.' I was immediately clean. Anything I had done was wiped away, and I was made new.

"I was taken through many levels and educated about life and the truth of how it is. A total education in the absolute truth of how it is. After we die, based on our relationship with the Supreme Being, we move forward, we go on. We may take another form or state, but I retained the same spirit. I was still me. We may or may not have the same body, but we have the same essence. It moved well beyond any religion.

"It changed my life. I requested to come back to raise that child because of what I'd learned. The Supreme Being is a he/she embracing all forms of life. Use me for a vessel, I said. Anything you want. My request was honored.

"This Supreme Being seems to place me in circumstances where people are dying. I'm privileged to be in the presence of many who need to be shown the rightness of leaving the body. I can walk down the hallway and feel God call me into a room and say, 'This person needs loving guidance.' I may step inside a doorway and I'll be totally obedient to what the Supreme Being wants me to do. I'm just a vessel."

While not all near-death experiences (NDEs) include this sense of prophetic anointment, Judge's narrative resembles many other NDEs in almost all points. Raymond Moody, a philosophy and psychology professor at a university in eastern North Carolina, was the first person to gather and publish narratives of NDEs and the first to use the phrase "near-death experience." His book, *Life After Life*, originally published in 1975, surveyed the individual experiences of some fifty people who had survived an NDE. The book, which was a best-seller, begins with a composite NDE, one that, Moody wrote, "embodies all of the common elements in the order in which it is typical for them to occur." He added that none of the elements in his composite occurred in all the NDEs, but they all occurred in a number of them.

In Moody's paradigmatic NDE, at the moment of death, a man is pronounced dead by the doctors and nurses around him. He hears a loud buzzing or ringing in his ears and find himself moving through a long, dark tunnel. He then finds himself in the same room where he has died, but watching his body and others move around it as if from above or at a distance. He has a body but it is "of a different nature" than the one he had during his life. "He glimpses the spirits of relatives and friends who have already died, and a loving warm spirit of a kind he has never experienced before—a being of light—appears before him," wrote Moody. "This being asks him a question, non-verbally, to make him evaluate his life and helps him along by showing him a panoramic, instant playback of the major events of his life. . . . He is overwhelmed by intense feelings of joy, love, and peace."

At some point, and much to the disappointment of the person undergoing the NDE, he or she understands that it is not yet the moment to die and that a return to the body left behind is required. The experience is wholly real, and often substantiated by a patient being able to recall what those around the body were doing while the person experiencing the NDE was unconscious, or to recount what the doctors and nurses were saying, impossible for a dying person or someone under anesthesia to have known. The final common experience that these people have is that the NDE profoundly changes them for the rest of their lives by eliminating any fear they may have had about dying and providing them with an abiding certainty that there is life after death.

Moody was only twenty-six years old, a young philosophy

professor in eastern North Carolina, when he began gathering cases of NDEs. The first book generated many more reports from those who had experienced an NDE and never spoken about it as well as from doctors and nurses who had heard patients narrate them. It soon became a recognized fact that some people do have these kinds of experiences when they are at death's door, and that they are basically similar—all see a bright light, for instance—although people from different religious backgrounds will have a different picture of the being who talks to them.

"Stories of people who return from death, bringing back eyewitness testimony about the other world, can be found in nearly every religious tradition; and although they have many similar features, such reports invariably portray this experience in ways that conform to cultural expectations," writes Carol Zaleski in her essay about NDEs, "Death and Near-Death Today."

Raymond Moody's book, in addition to generating a new aspect of medicine and thanatology, brought down considerable criticism on its author's head. Some of the strongest came from Paul Edwards who pointed out in *Reincarnation: A Critical Examination* that none of the people quoted at length from Moody's pool of fifty NDE survivors is identified. Moody, claiming that he will not violate the total confidentiality of these reports, has consistently refused to open his files to even one or two investigators so that his findings could be corroborated.

In addition, Moody's own belief trajectory has been an

unusual one, to say the least. Following his research into NDEs, he obtained a medical degree and began practicing psychiatry, using hypnotic past-life regression as his primary analytical tool. His latest book is *Reunions: Visionary Encounters with Departed Loved Ones*, in which he provides instructions whereby anyone can contact dead relatives simply by using a large mirror in a specially arranged room, which he calls an "apparition chamber."

It has sold briskly, but nothing like *Life After Life*, which sold three million copies between 1975 and 1978. Moody's book initiated a widening awareness of NDEs, and reports began to come in from around the world. In publications ranging from learned journals to cheap paperbacks for reading on airplanes, writers, scientists, doctors, psychologists, and parapsychologists weighed in on the question, to say nothing of those who had died and come back to life. It turns out that there are a lot of people who say they have approached death's door, stepped through, and come back to talk about it. The fact that many people *do* undergo the sort of paradigmatic experience related by Moody is now accepted without question. For some people, even if they have not personally lived the experience, the knowledge that many have done so is a reassurance about immortality, although not everyone, not even all of those who believe in eternal life, finds the vision brought back by NDEs reassuring.

Evangelical Christians find the tales difficult to accept, because they sound too good to be true. For someone who believes in a final judgment and the reality of eternal damnation for sinners, it does not seem right that nonbelievers as well as true Christians have this beautiful experience waiting for them after death. After all, for those who are not saved, dying is not something to be anticipated; it is not going to be filled with reassuring bright light and joy. Hell is hardly a pleasing prospect.

Maurice Rawlings, a physician in Chattanooga, Tennessee, and a fundamentalist Christian who claimed to have had his own NDE following a heart attack, decided that many cases had to exist of people who had gotten a foretaste of hell instead of heaven, and he dug out a few narratives for his book *To Hell and Back*, published in 1993 by Thomas Nelson, the nation's leading evangelical publisher. Rawlings claimed to have found evidence of some fifty cases in which people near death were indescribably happy to be brought back to life, rescued from the terrible visions they were having in their NDEs. None of the usual how-they-regretted-returning-to-their-bodies, but instead people who were ecstatically happy to feel pain and be alive. His book, however, is more an attack from an evangelical Christian on the New Age than a record of individual negative NDEs, and his journalistic and scientific accomplishments are even fewer than Moody's.

NDEs are of interest to a number of disciplines, including neuroscience and psychiatry. That people experience them is currently accepted, but the underlying question of what they are and why they are happening remains unanswered. That an NDE is a possible experience of *dying* is, apparently, indisputable, but it is not so easy to argue that it is an experience of *death*. No one who is known to have had an NDE was irreversibly, biologically dead, and the fact that NDEs happen does not prove the existence of an individual soul, something separate from the body, nor can it count as evidence that something awaits us after death.

For many, the physical explanation of what happens during an NDE is the most convincing. A combination of reduced oxygen intake and a massive release of endorphins and perhaps other feel-good chemicals manufactured by our own bodies serves to palliate the pain and fear of death as the body shuts down. However, in a careful analysis of the evidence and writings about NDEs in his 2003 book *Religion, Spirituality and the Near-Death Experience*, Mark Fox concluded that they remain, for now, a mystery and that neither science nor theology is able to account fully for all the phenomena common to patient reports. He leaves open the possibility that medicine and science will one day be able to explain them fully, and also admits that it may one day be concluded they were only one more tiny manifestation of the human race's struggle to explain death on purely hypothetical and hysterical grounds.

Nevertheless, the neuroscientific version has numerous adherents who attribute NDEs to strictly physical causes. "The production of endorphins leads to a total relaxation of the muscles," writes the German molecular biologist Mark Benecke in *The Dream of Eternal Life*. "This is why mice, once caught, hang limply in the jaws of their feline predators.

"The pleasant floating feeling described by some who have narrowly escaped death stems from the same muscle-relaxing endorphins produced by the body. Even the feelings of happiness and contentment that have been felt by nearly all people who have 'returned' from death could possibly be a result of such substances. . . .

"When the body nearing death releases such 'drugs' into the bloodstream to suppress pain or to relax the musculature and the mind, the total cooperation of mind and body takes place for the last time. Such a death is peaceful and mild."

Perhaps we share with the animal world a mechanism to protect ourselves from extreme pain in our last moments, which comes into play for an animal being devoured by a lion, for instance, whether that animal is antelope or human. In his book *The Songlines*, the late writer and traveler Bruce Chatwin quotes another writer and traveler from a century earlier, African explorer Stanley Livingstone, who survived being mauled by a lion. "It causes," wrote Livingstone in *Missionary Travels*, "a kind of dreaminess in which there was no sense of pain nor feeling of terror. It was what patients under chloroform describe who see all the operation but not the knife. . . . This particular state is probably produced in all animals killed by the carnivores; and, if so, is a merciful provision by our benevolent creator for lessening the pain of death."

It is possible that a prey animal is overcome by a release of chemicals that sends it into a predeath state of shock, minimizing discomfort and fear. If this is the case, is it not probable that if we lie broken, bleeding out our lives on a highway beside a crumpled car, the same mechanism will ease our final moments? Perhaps a chemical reaction is programmed into our cells, a formula that kicks in to make the inevitable easier as we die. At this moment, perhaps the near-death experience is initiated by our bodies, accompanied by images that depend on cultural conditioning.

"Therefore," writes Benecke, "it is entirely possible that the body releases hormones in our moments closest to death, and these hormones may play on our nervous systems so that they help to conjure up the images so often and repetitively described. These death motifs, one might imagine, are a kind of thought pattern already inscribed, chemically or hormonally, in the human body. They need only be retrieved, especially in extreme circumstances."

What this hypothesizes is that mercy is built into our genome. We hope so. We doubt it.

❧

NDEs are nothing new, writes Harold Bloom in his *Omens of Millennium*, published in 1996. "The 'near-death experience' is another pre-Millennium phenomenon that travesties Gnosticism; every account we are given of this curious matter culminates in being 'embraced by the light,' by a figure of light known to Gnostic tradition variously as 'the astral body,' the 'Resurrection Body' or Hermes, our guide in the land of the dead."

In the early Middle Ages, according to Jon Brenner in *The Rise and Fall of the Afterlife*, visionary reports from those who had traveled beyond, to hell or Paradise, were common. Brenner highlights two, one from the Venerable Bede (circa 700 CE), and the other of the monk of Wenlock, as related by Boniface at around the same time. Each tells a tale of the worlds that await us after death, with visions of heavens and hell, and in each the traveler is required to return to his body, although each longs to remain in Paradise. "Both of these reports display some aspects of both classical and modern NDEs," concludes Brenner.

Written two thousand years before the Venerable Bede, the epic of Gilgamesh is in itself an NDE, a journey to the land of the dead. While positing that in some way we live on after death, little hope is held out in Gilgamesh that anything pleasant awaits us. It is gray and it is endless. From this ancient vision a postmortem existence emerged that was not appealing but was the first of many descriptions of the afterworld and the mechanisms of dying. Many others followed it. Such documents run an ample spectrum between the *Tibetan Book of the Dead* and Dante's *Divine Comedy*. To say nothing of Moody's *Life After Life* and the hundreds of books published each year purporting to tell us what happens when we die.

Who knows to what extent *The Divine Comedy* allowed Dante Alligheri to put bread on his family's table, or how many Tibetan monks recording the *Bardo Thödrol* were sustained with daily rations and shelter by the faithful over the years that they labored at their texts? The afterlife, for all its uncertainty, has always provided an income in *this* life for some people—a large income in some cases.

The publication of Moody's first book more or less coincided with the creation and growth in the United States of the New Age movement. This is an umbrella designation for believers in many different things, ranging from tarot cards to trance mediums, but all of whom would agree that a nonphysical component of each of us survives our individual deaths. The New Age is a network of people—mostly white and of European ancestry—who believe in the transforming power of faith, the transcendent nature of the soul, but do not find that traditional religion works for them. It was not difficult to fit NDEs into the cosmology embraced by New Age believers.

Repackaging and selling the old truths in cheap, popularized formats has always generated profits, and while the New Age movement has probably diverted billions of dollars from the offering plates of the more established faiths, luring their flocks and funds away, it has simultaneously created its own market, a vast network of people subscribing to a new belief system. Harold Bloom describes this marketplace as offering up a "travesty of ancient verities," cheap knockoffs tailored to the marketplace. NDEs are nothing more than another industry designed for the consumer, using the ancient Gnostic teachings. He writes:

"Industry it certainly has become, just as the purveyors of angels are a growth item. We now have IANDS (the International Association for Near-Death Studies) which offers maroon T-shirts, and features a logo that intermixes Moody's tunnel with the Taoist emblem of yin and yang. The quarterly put-out is called *Vital Signs*; there are workshops, conventions, study groups, and much else. This sounds rather like a novel by Aldous Huxley or even Evelyn Waugh, but is merely another instance of American millennial hysteria."

Well, hysteria maybe. But "American" and "millennial" don't sound quite right. At all times, in all places, someone can be found earning a bit of bread by pretending to some holiness or other, proving their grasp of the divine will by explaining what happens when people die. Religious and spiritual manipulation of the gullible to relieve them of their cash has turned up as often around the globe as weeds grow in a garden. A run-of-the-mill shaman has to eat like anyone else, as does a preacher, monk, or snake-oil salesman. Some of them eat a lot.

What is true is that the market for religious notions has never been more ample or potentially lucrative than in today's consumerist First World culture, the "me culture," in which individuals participate less and less in their communities, with each family unit closed away behind its doors, connected to the world by virtual means outside of any ecclesiastical structure. It is a culture with a large market for snake-oil salesmen, online and in the real world. The twentieth century was a barbarous and precarious time, Apocalypse seemed imminent, and many former Jews and Christians found they could not accept the traditional monotheistic idea of one Supreme Being intentionally directing all the lives in the world, with eternity, forever spent in heaven or hell depending on what we have done in this one life ("It is appointed unto men once to die, but after this the judgment." Hebrews 9:27). For many people, it was too difficult to imagine a God who could create and sanction this sort of world.

Post–World War II times seemed to call for a more relativistic, syncretic approach to religion. If two thousand years of monotheism had produced so little change in humanity that war and cruelty continued as history's keynote, many felt it was time to begin searching for ways to explain the world other than those offered by mainstream religions. By the end of the 1960s, Christians were beginning to leave their mainline churches for smaller, more conservative, evangelical congregations. People were also beginning to form a network—and a marketplace—of New Age believers.

There is little about New Age thought that is in fact new. J. Gordon Melton, founder and director of the Institute for the Study of American Religion, makes precisely this point in an essay about New Age believers and beliefs, "Beyond Millennialism: The New Age Transformed." He echoes Bloom in reminding readers that astrology, meditation, channeling, reincarnation, and numerous other aspects of New Age culture reincorporate beliefs that have persisted for millennia. Believers in these ancient divination practices and those searching for something more acceptable than the wrath of a montheistic God were brought together for the first time under the New Age umbrella. A New Age is upon us, just about to unfold, a time in which spiritual transformation will make us happy, realized individuals and create world peace. "The heart of the New Age has been interaction around the different tools of spiritual transformation," writes Melton.

The name New Age was coined to describe people engaged in alternative spiritual practices and came to include those following alternative physical practices as well: from holistic health practitioners to chiropractors. The growth in numbers of people who identified themselves as New Age believers has been substantial. Surveys ten years apart by the American Religious Identification Study, carried out by the Graduate Center of the City University of New York, showed that in 1991, more people considered themselves Scientologists than New Agers, but in 2001 that situation had reversed. The numbers of Scientologists had grown, but only slightly, while over three times as many survey respondents identified themselves as New Age adherents than ten years previously. The name New Age also refers to the primary conviction among believers that a new age is dawning, a new millennium that will usher in a more spiritual era in which both individuals and societies will be transformed.

Melton asserts that the popularity of New Age beliefs peaked through the 1980s, then went into a slow decline based on the fact that the radically changed world promised by the New Age did not happen. A succession of dates was posited, beginning with the "Harmonic Convergence" in 1987, in which drastic changes would take place on earth and among its peoples. When these failed to materialize, writes Melton, the movement lost its momentum. Nevertheless, it was not quite ready to be relegated to the status of a blip on the map of strange religious fervors that stretch back for millennia. "The transition of the 1990s, in the wake of the disappointment that the New Age had failed to make an appearance, has allowed the gains of the 1980s to be consolidated," wrote Melton. "Under a variety of names, the older occult community has been established as an alternative faith community (or more precisely a set of alternative communities) which share a common hope for their own prosperity in the next century as well as their meaningful role in the evolution progress of humanity.

"The New Age may have died, but the community it brought together continues to grow as one of the most important minority faith communities in the West. While showing no signs of assuming the dominant religious role in the West, it is reclaiming and resacralizing a small part of the secularized world. . . ."

One way in which the New Age movement has profoundly affected daily life in the developed world is through its influence on the idea of holistic medicine and a patient taking responsibility for his or her well-being, including the use of "alternative" therapies. The idea is that when an individual falls ill with a disease or chronic condition, treatment needs to be tailored to the individual as a whole person and with his or her participation. These kinds of ideas, once an anathema to physicians and unrecognized by the medical establishment, are now being discussed in medical schools around the country, and some of the nation's best hospitals are bringing alternative therapy practitioners into their precincts. The absolute hegemony of doctors over their patients has modified over the past few decades, a trend that New Age health practitioners have influenced.

Not everyone agrees that this constitutes a positive service. Columnist and illusionist/magician Henry Gordon, a strident skeptic, whose books are published by Prometheus, points to the people whose trust in these practices discourages them from seeking timely traditional medical help. Gordon does not deny that some alternative therapies can help some people some of the time, but complains that they are largely unregulated and undocumented. "Of all the potential harmful effects that can be laid on the doorstep of the New Age movement, I would say that the current promotion of alternative medical practice is the most damaging," he writes in his 1988 book *Channeling into the New Age*:

"I am referring here to a great variety of practices: holistic medicine; chiropractic; naturopathy; homeopathy; acupuncture; hypnotherapy; health food fads; rolfing; reflexology; herbal medications; biofeedback; chelation therapy; iridology; therapeutic touch; vitamin megadoses; visualization therapy for cancer; crystal therapy; color therapy; body aura cures; and many others."

In 2005, these same conflicting points of view focused around what medicine calls Attention Deficit Disorder (ADD) or Attention Deficit Hyperactivity Disorder (ADHD) and what New Agers call the phenomena of Indigo children. Doctors regard ADD as a behavioral disease, treat it with Ritalin, and attribute its causes to a number of things from junk food to pollution. The numbers of ADD and ADHD children have risen dramatically in the past two decades, and some observers estimate there are more than two million in the United States alone. Many such children are identified early on and placed immediately on medication, and some spend more than a decade taking Ritalin. While the pharmaceutical, which bears a chemical resemblance to amphetamines, does work in most cases, allowing the kids to concentrate in class and control their impulsive behaviors, its long-term effects are not yet documented.

New Age believers, unlike doctors and teachers, do not see these children as having a problem but rather view them as an evolutionary step forward for the human race. They are called Indigo children, because indigo is the color associated with the coming new age, according to Nancy Ann Tappe, who claims in her writings and interviews that some 90 percent of children born today are Indigo. Their evolved personality traits and higher understanding make it hard for them to function in the old, outmoded world, according to Lee Carroll and Jan Tober, authors of *The Indigo Child*. They assert that such children are often misdiagnosed with ADD. The New Age point of view may eventually generate studies and data to show that what looks like a new and spreading problem of juvenile health is in reality a blessing for the affected children and the world in which they live. Is diet, television, the air they breathe, or the water they drink causing their brains or bodies to malfunction? Are they victims of an environmental illness that robs them of their capacity to pay attention and respond appropriately to the world around them? Or are these children emissaries of a new stage in human development, representatives of our future, intuitive and psychic, presumably more peaceful and cooperative? It may be that New Age resistance to the pharmaceutical approach will play a role in deciphering the problem by creating a control group of affected youngsters who do not take Ritalin.

Another way in which New Age believers changed the modern medical establishment was by insisting that death was a medical topic and that medical professionals needed to cope with it. Elisabeth Kübler-Ross's best-selling book *On Death and Dying*, did everyone the favor of making death a discussable, teachable, and respectable topic. Because of her ideas about lessening the suffering and anxiety that death engenders, she was listened to by doctors and nurses around the world, and because of her beliefs about what happens after death—Ross was a firm believer in reincarnation—she was embraced and fervently promoted by the New Age network.

It is difficult to accept J. Gordon Melton's thesis that the New Age has peaked if one includes among its number those people who are following some sort of alternative physical practice or therapy in their daily lives. It was New Age believers who often expressed initial interest in and acceptance of these various practices, and today they are used by multitudes and generate tremendous amounts of money. For instance, an article in *Yoga Journal* by Russell Wild estimated that 19 million people in the United States alone practice yoga, and the revenues associated with it amount to more than $25 billion annually. The American Herbalist's Guild estimated in 1999 that the herbal extract industry had some $4.5 billion in annual sales.

The vitamin and food supplement business is huge. The online purveyor Vitamin World manufactures over a thousand such products, ranging from things most Westerners would recognize, like vitamin C, to things many might not have heard of, potions such as gelcaps containing alpha lipoic acid or coenzyme Q10, both of which are listed on Vitamin World's Web site as effective antioxidants that rejuvenate the skin and help to retard the aging process on a cellular level. The site also notes that these claims are as yet untested scientifically. Vitamin World is a brand produced by NBTY, Inc., which trades on the NASDAQ stock exchange as NBTY. The company reported third-quarter sales in 2004–2005 of some $439 million.

Of course, it is not only New Age religion that sells well—many of the older more traditional religions also have healthy bottom lines at the end of the year. Whether it is New Age or Old Age, it is a fact that religion sells. In his article, Wild points out that Christianity, too, is a large business, with the Bible and "Christian" books generating $1.8 billion in 2002 sales.

Around 40 percent of U.S. adults consistently respond when surveyed that at some point in their lives they have been in contact with someone who is dead, so it is not surprising that New Agers adopted, pretty much of whole cloth, the beliefs of what Melton called the "older occult community." These stretch back in an unbroken line deep into the nineteenth-century parlors of Victorian England, where the dead were summoned to seances, and from there, with various zigs and zags, perhaps as far back as prehistory, back to the times when divination was practiced by gifted individuals who rolled bones or read entrails. The basic idea that the dead can communicate with and advise the living is an ancient one.

The practice of communicating with the dead has proven highly adaptable to modern marketing techniques used by contemporary practitioners. The hand-lettered sign in the window announcing "Psychic Readings" still exists, but client recruitment also takes place on the Internet, on pay television, and in the Yellow Pages, all means of getting hands in the wallets of the desperate and the credulous. New Age believers have proven a particularly fertile ground for flim-flam, vulnerable to a hustle that is hard for some people to resist perpetrating, particularly those who like attention, acclaim, and "easy" money. In the United States, the history of this sort of psychic grifter is often said to have originated with the Fox sisters. At least, it was the first time the media seems to have played what was to be its typical role—first publicizing something as amazing, and later debunking it.

The Fox sisters, Margaret and Katie, were from upstate New York and made a name for themselves in the mid-1800s while they were still young girls. They discovered that by snapping their big toes on the floor, they could make a "rapping" sound, which they learned to project into different parts of a room. People began to believe the girls were communicating with the spirits of the dead, and the sisters made no attempt to discourage such hypotheses. Life must have been boring in Hydesville, New York, and this was a pleasing way of passing the time and bringing in egg money as well. The sisters devised a code whereby people could ask them questions and receive answers in various forms of rappings. Neighbors and then the local newspapers spread the word about what was happening. Eventually the family moved to Rochester, New York, and the fame of the Fox sisters spread as far as England.

Then, in 1888, Margaret Fox published a confession in the *New York World* newspaper. She explained the trick and laid the blame at the door of an older sister, Leah, and her mother. "We were led on by my sister purposely and by my mother unintentionally," she wrote. "We often heard her say, 'Is this a disembodied spirit that has taken possession of my dear children?' "

Years later, Margaret Fox was to retract the confession in the *World*, saying she had been pressured to write it. At the time, however, she was certainly explicit. "I think it is about time that the truth of this miserable subject 'Spiritualism' should be brought out," she confessed, as quoted in Henry Gordon's *Channeling into the New Age*. "It is now widespread all over the world, and unless it is put down soon it will do great evil. I was the first in the field and I have the right to expose it."

In the last half of the nineteenth century, spiritism also found fertile ground in the United Kingdom. Queen Victoria consulted mediums with as much avidity as Ronald and Nancy Reagan would display a hundred years later in the White House, when they took care to hear from Nancy's favorite astrologer before making important decisions, according to aide Donald Regan in his kiss-and-tell book about them, *For the Record*. The queen believed she was able to communicate with her dead husband, Prince Albert, according to Herbie Brennan in his book *Death*. In Victorian England, seances and mediums were widely accepted, and the queen had frequent recourse to mediums, particularly after Prince Albert's death. The Society for Psychical Research was formed in 1882 in England and began a systematic investigation of channeling, telepathy, ESP, ghosts, and other psychic phenomenon. Among the founding members of the society was Sir William Crookes, said by some to be the most eminent British scientist of his day. The society still exists and maintains an extensive archive of psychic phenomena.

Across the Atlantic, some highly respected scientific minds believed it was possible to communicate with the dead.

Thomas Edison, for example, believed he would eventually develop electrical equipment allowing him to speak with the dead, of whose existence he entertained no doubts, according to Brennan. One person who bridged both sides of the Anglo-Saxon world was Eileen Garrett. Born in Ireland, she became famous when she predicted an English dirigible crash, which happened in 1930 over France. Her talent was for channeling the spirits of the dead. In 1931 she moved to the United States, where she was well received, prospered, and, in addition to giving private readings, spent a lot of time at various universities where scientists were investigating paranormal phenomena. In 1951, Garrett founded the Parapsychology Foundation in New York City. She was an intellectual who was uncertain about the sources of her psychic insights, wrote Fred Frohock in *Lives of the Psychics*. She was never certain whether the spirit guides who "controlled" her were truly the spirits of long-dead people or whether they were figments of her own unconscious.

Garrett's own public questioning of her abilities is rare. Those who can channel the dead—or believe they can, or simply maintain that they can—have a lot of temptations to resist. A decent annual income stands to be made as an intermediary between the dead and the living. Queen Victoria was by no means the only well-off woman who was willing to pay handsomely to have a medium on retainer. A pipeline to the other side is something for which people are often willing to pay a high price. It is a strong draw, and by no means only for women.

Sir Oliver Lodge was a leading British scientist, born in 1851, whose work in electromagnetic waves broke new scientific ground, and who also invented the system of electric spark ignition for internal combustion engines. He was knighted by King Edward VII in 1902 and lived until 1940. An august, tall, handsome man, he was the very image of a scientist using the tools of reason to unlock the mysteries of the universe. However, Lodge was also a strong believer in things unseen—he was an original member of the British Society for Psychical Research and he carried on many investigations into the paranormal with his friend Sir Arthur Conan Doyle, best known for his detective books about Sherlock Holmes. When Lodge's son Raymond died as a young soldier in 1915, during the World War I, Lodge's interest in spiritism deepened. He became convinced that he was able to communicate, virtually at will, with his dead son's spirit.

Fifty years later, the same kind of grief and longing motivated James Pike, a bishop in the U.S. Episcopal Church, to arrive at the heretical conclusion that he, too, was able to communicate with his dead son. In 1968, Pike published a book, *The Other Side*, in which he detailed his belief in mediums and their ability to communicate with the dead. Pike was a man with impressive credentials. He was the head of the Department of Religion at Columbia University and dean of the Cathedral of Saint John the Divine in New York City. In 1966, his twenty-year-old son killed himself in a New York hotel room. He had a history of mental instability and drug use, and had been living with his father in the months preceding his suicide. Guilt and grief stand out clearly in Pike's book, he is a man clearly unmoored by the loss of his son and an easy believer, desperate for reassurance.

As Pike began to speak and write publicly about his experiences communicating with his dead son through mediums, he effectively ended his career possibilities in the Episcopal Church, but his books were best-sellers, and his story became well known. In September 1967, he made an appearance on Canadian television with a famous medium from the United States named Arthur Ford. Afterward, Pike spoke of how impressed he was by the things that Ford knew about his family, and his statement that he believed Ford had communicated with his dead son during the program appeared in newspapers around the world. Later, it was revealed that Ford had extensive files on the Pike case and had studied the family in depth. It is the same story time after time. A famous psychic is exposed, usually after a lifetime of fame and wealth. Skeptics crow triumphantly, and believers have their trust betrayed once again.

Perhaps, next to this world of fakirs and fakers is a parallel world of people who speak with the dead for free because they cannot help it, who cure simply because they can do so, but they can only do so if they don't charge for it. If these gifts of healing and mediumship exist, it makes sense that they are talents money cannot buy. Family and friends are likely to know about a person's gift, the neighbors may view the person as someone good to turn to when advice is needed, but money does not enter the process. The ability to channel messages from the dead or to heal the sick might be something that just happens to people, a gift or a curse, depending on how people view it, but something they have always had. They carry on with living their daily lives, go to work every day, and every so often they turn to the dead for counsel or assistance on their own or someone else's behalf. And every so often, the dead respond. Maybe it is like that—always something the gifted noticed when they were young children a capacity to see beyond what appears. They can never charge for it.

"In the primitive societies I have visited, there is often some sort of gift left by the person coming to consult the shaman. But in the modern Western world, I have come to the conclusion that anyone who makes their living using psychic powers is probably a fake," Stanley Krippner told me, over dinner in October 2005. He has written extensively on primitive healers, along with other books and articles on a variety of psychic phenomena, and is recognized as one of a small group of academic researchers hoping to generate empirical experimental data to support their beliefs in things like channeling and speaking with the dead. At seventy-two, Krippner travels around the world speaking to conferences in locations as far apart as Beijing and Sao Paolo.

Anyone who asks for money in return for the use of their "gift" is the psychic equivalent of a professional television wrestler, he said. If so, lots of potential paying customers are out there willing to pay vast sums of money for the show. People like James Randi, a former stage magician whom Stanley Krippner claims for a friend, have dedicated their lives to exposing the many ways in which mediums fleece the public. Their efforts, while illuminating, do not seem to have diminished the willingness of many to spend their money in hopes of communicating with the dead. A former medium named M. Lamar Keene wrote a book in 1997, *The Psychic Mafia*, also published by the relentlessly skeptical Prometheus Books, in which he detailed his life among the mediums at a place called Camp Chesterfield in Indiana, where the faithful came to spend their vacations and their money each summer, going from medium to medium. The psychics were housed and fed by the colony's owner, who took a commission for every reading given. Other such vacation spots exist around the country.

Professional mediums all over the world are eager to talk about how many of their colleagues are fakes. "There are a couple of ways to determine if a psychic is genuine or not," said Mary Bogart, who charges thirty dollars for a half-hour "consultation" in Nashville. "A genuine psychic will never try to get you to come back. You come to me for a reading, you sit here for thirty minutes, you pay me thirty dollars, you go home and you're done. I don't want to waste my time reading you again unless something pretty drastic has changed in your life."

Bogart, thirty-eight, sees her clients in a small cubicle off the back hallway of a New Age bookstore in a Nolensville

Road strip mall at the southern edge of the city. A couple of folding chairs and a small table with an incense holder fill the space. She wears a crystal on a thin gold chain around her neck. She is tall, with long blonde hair, blue eyes, thin fingers; she is a former insurance adjuster who was "down-sized" out of a job and has been giving readings full-time for only a few months, but she has had psychic abilities ever since she can remember:

"Another way to tell if someone's genuine is that they'll tell you things that are specific. They don't have to tell you things you want to hear, that's different, but somebody who just goes, "Hmm, you've done well in business, you work hard, you have issues with your mother. . . ." I want to hear more detail than that."

Bogart never knows who a day will bring to the door of her cubicle, which she leaves open when she is inside with a client. Some days, she said, she does fifteen or twenty readings and other days no one shows up. "All I do is just ask the other side. I say, 'I'm here and whoever you bring to me that's who I'm supposed to read.' You know? Because the other side has made it clear I'm doing what I should be doing. I've only been doing it full-time since August, and I've already done a television show; I've already, you know, been interviewed for the local morning show. My spirit guides have told me I'm going to write several books."

What happens when we die? It is the same for all of us, she said, believers and nonbelievers, alike. The soul leaves the dead body and goes on. "That's the energy I feel, it's just an energy that keeps going on. From what I can see, there's a lot of levels to the other side. Angels and archangels. When you cross over they're all thrilled that you're back. They call coming into life, 'death,' because being in this world is so negative. They call crossing back over, 'being born again.'

"You'll see I'm right, when you die if not before, but I can't take credit for it because it's all the other side. This is not me speaking. All I am is just a mouthpiece for them. That's it."

It is the same thing that Jean Ann Gilhead says. She is a fifty-seven-year-old Englishwoman from just outside London who has lived in Barcelona for more than a decade. Over her lifetime, she told me, she has communicated with the dead "thousands" of times. "It has nothing to do with me; I'm just the vessel through which it passes, I connect the two sides and nothing more."

Gilhead, fifty-seven, cannot remember a time when she was not surrounded by spirits. Her grandmother, Winnie Rutherford, was a medium in the 1920s and 1930s among the "pioneers," Gilhead told me when I spoke with her in the living room of her modest Barcelona flat high in the hills, with a spectacular view of the city and the Mediterranean below. She lives there alone. Her mother is eighty-five and practices psychic healing in a center in London. Gilhead is an interior designer who specializes in using feng shui—a Chinese system of energy alignment—in designing a room or a building. She is also a medium, an aura reader, and a healer with a small but devoted clientele:

"We don't die, there's no such thing as dead. We just move from one energy state to another, we are a mind energy that never stops, the personality continues from one to another but it changes, too. In that sense we are immortal."

She has been shown and told these things over the years by her spirit guides. She has no other powers except that of receiving the energy of these guides, but it is sufficient to accomplish many things, including healing the sick or suffering. "When I'm healing, I call on my healing guides. It's just the transference of energy from my guide through me, through my physical body, and into the person I'm giving the healing to. That's all it is. I'm not actually doing anything, I'm just a channel."

It is a mild, Anglo-Saxon, New Age form of possession, but possession nonetheless, taken over by a spirit, a visitor from beyond the grave, invisible to the eyes of the living but there all the while. It can be summoned. Money usually changes hands. She sees nothing wrong with someone being compensated for the time it takes to channel or to heal, she told me.

A much ruder kind of possession is that practiced in the foothills of eastern Tennessee's Smoky Mountains. In 1975, I attended a worship service with a congregation of people who handled rattlesnakes and drank strychnine in their small, one-room church, the Church of the Holy Ghost with Signs Following, led by a preacher named Liston Pack. They were poor people, scratching out a living in the hollows of the foothills of the Great Smoky Mountains. The church was on a hillside in a piece of deep woods in Cocke County, the most lawless county in Tennessee, where unemployment was traditionally high, and the best opportunity for making some money was contraband—making whiskey in a still in the old days, or growing a cash crop of weed these days. Believers in Cocke County tend to be fervent.

On Saturday afternoon, half a dozen of the men in the church had gone out and trapped snakes, rattlers and copperheads, which they kept in wooden boxes with hinged lids. They were good at snake hunting, and it did not take them long to collect enough for the evening service. When the spirit of the Lord is all over them—what they call being "anointed"—the snake handlers can caress rattlesnakes and drink strychnine with perfect security, as I saw with my own eyes on that Saturday night. The parking lot outside the simple cement church was full. Inside was a high-octane energy. Some people were speaking in tongues. The rest of the congregation, about thirty people, were singing Hank Williams's soulful gospel song, "I Saw the Light"; they were clapping and praising the Lord. There was a power and shared ecstasy among them that sucked me right in and wrapped me up. I did not have any desire to go up front and pick a rattler up out of a box, but I felt no fear for those who were doing so, even though the tail rattles were whirring as the snakes were lifted into the air, rattling in a warning counterpoint to the clapping hands and raised voices. A presence surrounded the church, the air inside was charged with a rare and powerful feeling.

The snake handlers do not pick up the serpents until they feel themselves "anointed." The people who went up to the front of the church would wait a bit, then dip and put a hand into a wooden box on the floor with snakes inside, lift out a rattlesnake with its tail buzzing, and bring the snake's eyes up to an even level with their own. Then they would pass the snake, still buzzing with that frenetic threatening hum of rattles that makes any sane person want to back off as quickly as possible, to the man or woman beside them. All in keeping with Mark 16:15–18 in the New Testament, recording the words of Jesus in his charge to his disciples:

"Go ye into all the world, and preach the gospel to every creature. He that believeth and is baptized shall be saved; but he that believeth not shall be damned.

"And these signs shall follow them that believe; In my name shall they cast out devils; they shall speak with new tongues;

"They shall take up serpents; and if they drink any deadly thing, it shall not hurt them; they shall lay hands on the sick, and they shall recover."

Dying from the venom of a Tennessee timber rattler or from strychnine poisoning is not an easy death, but if one of Pack's congregants was bitten—and it happened occasionally —or took ill from a long drink of poison, he or she would often refuse medical attention in the belief that it was up to

God if they lived or died. Pack's own brother was such a case. "When my brother died, that was the last time I ever heard from my father. He's not a believer," Pack told me when I spoke to him after the service.

He was a pale man with a slight paunch and an air about him of living an intense, nearly unbearable faith. "Who can say why my brother died? God took him for His own reasons. Sometimes, for some reason, someone may decide to handle when they're not fully anointed. But you know it when you're anointed. You can't mistake it; you feel it when it comes on you."

His whole body went numb and disappeared when the Lord's anointing came down on him, Pack told me. He said it was impossible to describe the feeling any further. He was able to do so, however, for Thomas Burton, who interviewed Pack in his book, *Serpent-Handling Believers*. Pack told him how it felt to have God's protection come over you, when you knew you could handle serpents or drink poison. It was like having a stroke, he said; when it happened he lost all feeling beginning with his face. That's when he could comfortably move to the box with the snakes inside or take one from the person beside him. "Then I am fully anointed. I don't care where its head is, I don't care where its tail's at or the middle of it. I don't care where it's at and I'll handle it any way that I see fit. And that's about as close to the anointing that I can explain," he told Burton.

An equally rude possession is the one that overcomes

people in Afro-Caribbean religions. The dead and the spirit world can influence our world for good or bad. Contact with the other world is often achieved by giving up the body to a spirit, consenting to being taken. Here, too, as in eastern Tennessee, an altered state of consciousness is immediately evident in the traditional rites of such belief systems as Santería in Cuba and Vodoun in Haiti. People call it by different names, but to be present during such a possession is to witness another dimension of human experience coming into play. Something out of the ordinary is clearly happening. Regardless of where in the region they are found, or what they are called, the Afro-Caribbean religions all share some basic qualities, according to Margarite Fernández Olmos and Lizabeth Paravisini-Gebert in their book, *Creole Religions of the Caribbean*.

"Afro-Caribbean religions are centered on the principle of contact or mediation between humans and the spirit world, which is achieved through such numerous and complex rituals as divinatory practices, initiation, sacrifice, spiritual possession, and healings."

They go on to explain another of the common threads that bind the religions, which grew out of African beliefs brought to the Caribbean by the slaves and mixed with the Roman Catholicism of the colonial Europeans. "These religious practices are also linked by a cult of dead ancestors and/or deceased members of the religious community who watch over and influence events from beyond."

The spirits and the dead form a network among believers,

an infrastructure, a deep order in the universe, which infuses devotees' daily lives and actions with significance. Spirits influence their lives, and in dreams, in trance, in prayer, devotees can speak and listen to the dead. The visible world is not the only world, although it is the one they occupy. They must pay attention to the visible and invisible if they hope to enlist the support of the spirit world in helping their lives unfold satisfactorily, in smoothing the way ahead and protecting them. This is religion's principal task in their lives: to function as a bridge between the living and the other world.

To hold open the door. To crack our eggshell heads. To change ever so slightly the mechanism regulating what we notice and what we don't notice, a small tinkering with the brain's reticular activating system to change what it is we perceive and what slides by invisibly. Maybe that's all it takes to plug into the other world, the one our souls will recognize when we die. As there was room in this world for all of us alive right now, perhaps there's a next world waiting that also has room for all of us to pass through, again and again. Who remembers being born?

PART THREE
Oblivion

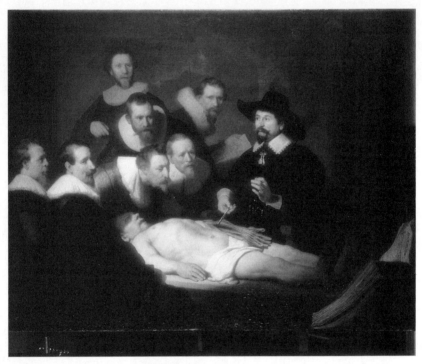

The Anatomy Lesson of Dr. Tulp, by Rembrandt. *Courtesy of the Royal Cabinet of Paintings, Mauritshuis, The Hague.*

5

The Nonbeliever's Faith

Love was the first to dream of immortality—not religion, not revelation. We love, therefore we wish to live.

Robert Ingersoll

I n 1968, a Gallup survey reported that 73 percent of Americans believed in life after death, 8 percent did not know, and 19 percent said there was no life after death. The number of nonbelievers was rising as the twentieth century drew to a close. A 1997 Gallup poll taken in the Unied States reported that 67 percent of people surveyed believed they would continue to exist in some form after they died, 8 percent did not know, and 25 percent did not believe in anything beyond the grave. One in every four people believed that when the heart stops and the brain dies, it is the end of life.

The world goes on and we do not.

For all the attractive, absurd, terrifying, or logical attempts to describe immortality and the mechanisms by which it might function, the most likely conclusion for many people is that no such thing exists and that when we die every last little bit of us disappears. Believers and non-believers alike simply cease to exist. Consciousness is an entirely chemical process, and when death halts chemical production, the power is switched off, shut down. Game over. Gone.

It remains to be seen. Or not seen. It is the latter alternative that is the hardest to accept. The possibility that we shall never know what happens when we die, because death instantly obliterates every last trace of us, seems grossly unfair. Indeed, Sigmund Freud insisted that it is impossible for people to accept the fact that they are going to die. "Our own death is indeed unimaginable, and whenever we make the attempt to imagine it we can perceive that we really survive as spectators," he wrote in "Thoughts on War and Death," a 1915 essay. "Hence the psychoanalytic school could venture on the assertion that at bottom no one believes in his own death, or to put the same thing another way, in the unconscious every one of us is convinced of his own immortality. . . ."

The tension between the reality before us, that everyone dies, and our subconscious conviction that we are immortal generates anxiety and fear. It is the same fear that we knew as infants in a state of total helplessness. We look to God and religion to protect us, much as we looked to our parents to do so when we were vulnerable babies, said Freud, an avowed atheist. (The word *atheist* comes from the Greek, *without a deity*.) Freud once described himself as a "godless Jew." In his book *The Future of an Illusion*, he called for people to give up their beliefs in a God or an afterlife, although he recognized that people could not do so easily.

"They will, it is true, find themselves in a difficult situation," he wrote. "They will have to admit to themselves the full extent of their helplessness and their insignificance in the machinery of the universe; they can no longer be the center of creation, no longer the object of tender care on the part of a beneficent Providence. They will be in the same position as a child who has left the parental house where he was so warm and comfortable. But surely infantilism is destined to be surmounted. Men cannot remain children forever. They must in the end go out into 'hostile life.' "

While unconsciously we may all believe that we shall live

forever, consciously, rationally, a quarter of those living in the United States believe that death is our final end. While James Reeves cannot imagine how he could face his mornings without believing in an afterlife, 25 percent of the nation's population are apparently able to live their daily lives untroubled by the prospect of oblivion, and they are able to make sense of their lives despite the prospect of personal extinction.

Just as important, many of them live by carefully elaborated moral guidelines. Believers often charge that nontheists, in addition to blighting their own lives and those of their children by persistently denying God's freely offered love and grace, have no reliable source for instruction about how to live on this earth, and are without firm moral guidelines like the golden rule and the ten commandments. They point to examples from recent history like Adolf Hitler and Josef Stalin as examples of atheism linked to evil in men wholly lacking a moral compass. These men are, however, no different from those who have pursued holy wars in the name of one belief or another down through the centuries. Lack of belief in a next world does not necessarily imply the absence of a strict moral code in this one. Just as believers and nonbelievers alike are capable of monstrous evil, so both are capable of the most beneficent good. The nonbelievers' principles and sense of justice, of how things *should* be, can motivate them to live lives in which harm done is held to a minimum, and help rendered at a maximum.

Some of the greatest minds down through the ages have concluded that when we die, we are dead and gone. The prospect did not seem to bother Aristotle or Albert Einstein, Epicurus or Karl Marx, Lucretius or David Hume, all of whom believed that nothing of us remained after death, and all of whom we still remember for their ideas and brilliant minds, although they, too, will one day be as forgotten as other great minds before them in civilizations gone to dust and wholly lost to us, great, vast histories and bustling cities disappeared as if they never were.

Alongside the names we still remember of those down through the millennia who went on record as not believing in an afterlife are the already forgotten multitudes, the one in every four ordinary people who do not think anything waits. Nontheists are not united by a single faith, they do not form a single community of nonbelievers, and individual atheists cannot usually trace their atheism back in history with as much facility as believers can recount the principal narrative of their religions, the life story of Christ, or Moses, or Mohammed, or the Buddha. Nevertheless, atheism has a history paralleling that of the great religions. The one in every fourth person who believes the biological process brings us forth and then we are done, has a doctrinal tradition every bit as old as any recorded religion's, populated with revolutionary thinkers, martyrs, and sages.

The first record of organized nontheism is from India, where it appeared sometime between 600 and 1000 BCE, before the Buddha lived. This materialistic school of thought was called Lokayata, which means "the world," and referred to people who counted on only what they could see. Lokayata had an identifiable founder named Brihaspati, but the only fragments of his teaching that survive are those quoted by various Vedantic writers, primarily for the purpose of refuting them. All of our records of Lokayata are secondhand. Original Lokayata texts are thought to have existed but to have been completely destroyed, probably by Hindu Brahmins, who are generally thought to have paid for the autos-da-fé. That would not be surprising, as Lokayata reserved its harshest criticism for the priestly, Brahmin ruling class with its "sacerdotal cunning." Among the texts cited are one referred to as the Brhaspati sutra:

No heaven exists, no final liberation,
No soul, no other world, no rites of caste . . .
The triple veda, triple self command,
And all the dust and ashes of repentance—
These yield a means of livelihood for men
Devoid of intellect and manliness . . .
How can this body when reduced to dust
Revisit earth? And if a ghost can pass
To other worlds, why does not strong affection
For those he leaves behind attract him back?
The costly rites enjoined for those who die
Are but a means of livelihood devised
By sacerdotal cunning—nothing more . . .
While life endures, let life be spent in ease

And merriment; Let a man borrow money
From all his friends, and feast on melted butter."

The two principal lines of ancient Indian belief were
Lokayata and the Vedantic system that developed into what
the West knows as Hinduism. The nontheist, materialistic
perspective descended from Lokayata was called Carvaka
by the time the Buddha lived, centuries later, and he was
well aware of it. His contemporary, Ajita Kesakambal, was
the best-known spokesman for what had begun with Brihaspati. Carvaka taught that humans live only once and
that the only true things are those of this world—no gods,
no heaven, no hell.

"There is no [merit in] almsgiving, sacrifice, or offering,
no result or ripening of good or evil deeds," Ajita is quoted
in Rhys Davids's translation of the Digha Nikaya, the *Dialogues of the Buddha*. "There is no passing from this world to
the next. . . . There is no afterlife. . . . Man is formed of four
elements: when he dies earth returns to the aggregate of the
earth, water to water, fire to fire, and air to air, while the
senses vanish into space. Four men take up the corpse; they
gossip as far as the burning ground, where his bones turn the
color of a dove's wing and his sacrifice ends in ashes."

Scholars believe that Lokayata was one of India's earliest
important belief systems and one commanding a significant
number of followers. The vehemence and frequency with
which they were jeered, refuted, and consigned to the dustbin
of thought by later scribes offer evidence that the Vedantic

writers viewed Lokayata as serious competition. Some scholars believe that Lokayata went through various stages, extending over possibly a thousand years, beginning, perhaps, with a rationalist, humanist belief in what could be perceived with the senses and finishing centuries later, long after the Buddha died, on a note of extreme hedonism, pursuing the pleasures of the flesh at all cost.

Since Lokayata first appeared, it is unlikely that materialism has ever been entirely absent from Indian soil, but its adherents have been few in number through most of recorded history. Today, there is still a thread of disbelief that runs through India—the large cities have atheist and humanist societies, and the Communist Party has a small presence—but it is a thin thread in a wide tapestry. A global study of 50,000 people, reported in a 2005 article by Sujatta Dutta Sachdeva in the *Times of India*, found that 87 percent of Indians defined themselves as "believers," making them the second most religious nation in the world behind the Philippines, where 90 percent believed. Globally, 25 percent of the people questioned said they were "not religious," while in India "not religious" accounted for only 9 percent.

Atheism in the West has its roots in that same culturally rich couple of centuries in which the Buddha was alive, Taosim and Confucianism were developing, and Plato and Socrates were espousing their ideas of a surviving soul. From the beginnings of its presence in Western thought, nontheism has been championed by those most concerned with scientific investigation and finding an explanation for the origins of life. James Thrower, in his book *Western Atheism*, quotes a list taken from A. B. Drachman's *Atheism in Pagan Antiquity* of pre-Socratic Greeks who were labeled atheists by others. It includes the names of Xenophanes, Anaxagoras, Diogenes of Apollonia, Hippo of Rhegium, Protagoras, Prodicus, Critias, and Diagoras of Melos.

Agnosticism, too, had its early adherents. Protagoras, a fifth-century-BCE philosopher, wrote, "Concerning the gods I am unable to discover whether they exist or not, or what they are like in form; for there are many hindrances to knowledge, the obscurity of the subject and the brevity of human life."

Protagoras, who lived from 480 to 410 BCE, was the best known of all the Sophist school of philosophers and was a realist in all things. Relativism was at the base of his beliefs. The Sophists were concerned with how people should live together and how communities should function. It was the world at hand that people needed to deal with. No evidence existed for any other. What we saw was what we got. "Man is the measure of all things," said Protagoras, an attitude that was sufficiently unwelcome in official Athens that he was charged with impiety. Fleeing Greece for Sicily, he never arrived, and is thought to have drowned in a shipwreck.

The first cogent rebuttal of the existence of divine beings, or life after death, comes from one of the earliest and most important of the Greek scientists, Democritus, who was born around 460 BCE. His science was learned from his teacher, Leucippos, the first to propose that all matter is made of atoms. Scientists versus theologians. From the beginnings of Western thought, nontheists believed it was possible to understand how life's machinery functions in the here and now, and theists maintained that an explanation waits beyond death. For some, it was impossible to believe the world in all its complexity was not elaborated and organized by a higher power. For others, the scientific explanation for the way the world worked, based on an atomic system, was sufficient. As early as 300 BCE, records show, human dissections were practiced already there were those who felt that life could be explained by using observation and experiment to decipher its secrets, and they were going about doing it. The gods had no part to play in the world as Leucipps and Democritus saw it. What existed was life or nothing.

Democritus, in ordering the atomic system of his teacher, was the first to construct a mechanistic world in which the machinery could be explained, a self-enclosed functioning system. He described the atoms as eternal and incorruptible, differing from one another in form and density, all moving in the vacuum of space. He concluded that a soul existed, also composed of atoms, which died when the body died. For Democritus, the soul corresponded to what we call consciousness; it was what allowed us to reason and to appreciate things like beauty, the unique human capacity we bring to our apprehension of the world.

A strong and articulated school of nonbelief stretches

back through the great classical philosophers and naturalists. Around 350 BC, Aristotle broke with his teacher Plato's contention that the individual soul was immortal. Aristotle taught that nothing of an individual survives death. Something does survive each person's passing, leaving the body at death, he wrote, but it is not personal. It is a bit of the divine consciousness, that which animates each person and makes us able to think and to reason. It is the soul, and at death it separates from the body and returns to its source, but nothing of our individual person lives on after death.

Epicurus, at virtually the same time, was less timidly declaring that neither the gods nor souls exist and that this life is our only opportunity. His conclusions were based on Democritus's atomic theory, which he believed held the key to life's mysteries. Even without the conviction that some sort of life existed after the grave, death should not frighten us, he wrote. "The most terrifying of evils, death, is nothing to us, since when we exist, death is not present. But when death is present, then we do not exist. It is nothing, then, either to the living or to the dead, since concerning the former it does not exist, and concerning the latter, they no longer exist."

Epicurus was not an isolated, eccentric voice. His vision of the world apparently found some receptive listeners among everyday Greeks. Death is nothing to fear, because when we are gone, we are gone. In his book *Life After Death*, Alan Segal quotes an Epicurean epitaph found on gravestones in ancient Greece: "I was not, and I came into being; I am not, and I do not suffer."

In addition to his observations based on atomic science, Epicurus was, apparently, the first Western philosopher to maintain that the presence of evil in the world was a clear indication that no divinity existed. Why evil exists is a question that believers, including Job, and nonbelievers have debated ever since, but no one in the millennia that followed Epicurus would put it any better than he did:

> Are the gods willing to prevent evil, but not able? Then they are not omnipotent.
> Are they able, but not willing? Then they are malevolent.
> Are they both able and willing? Then whence cometh evil?
> Are they neither able nor willing? Then why call them gods?

The nontheistic view of the world was handed down from teacher to student along with the theory of the atom, the primal component of all matter. Critias, Diagoras, and Epicurus subscribed to it, and three hundred years later the Roman poet Lucretius, in the first century BCE, was praising Epicurus's thinking as well as concluding for himself: "If the nature of the soul is immortal and makes its way into our body at the time of birth, why are we unable to remember besides the time already gone, and why do we retain no traces of past actions? If the power of the mind has been so completely changed, that all remembrance of past things is lost, that seems to me not to differ widely from death."

If the soul continues living but has no memory of its prior individual life, then what is the difference, asks Lucretius. Where is the consolation in that? Best to follow Epicurus's recipe: live well, avoid pain, take pleasure in the sweet things of life and those that bring tranquillity to our inner beings. Do not worry about dying: the fear of death can make our days here bitter, although it is certain that there is nothing to fear, because when we die we shall simply disappear.

This was not strictly a nontheistic point of view. It was possible to believe in God, even the Old Testament God, and not believe in a hereafter. Not long after the time in which Lucretius was writing, the Sadducees were governing the Jews in the Holy Land, collaborating with the Romans. No records of the Sadducees have been found, but from what was written by others about them, it is clear that they were observant Jews who followed the Ten Command-ments, recognized only the Pentateuch (the first five books of the Bible) as Scripture and the basis for all law, and were well read in the Greek and Roman classics. They believed the world moved in accordance with God's will, but they did not believe in a coming messiah nor in an eventual res-urrection. Death, for the Sadducees, was final, according to Paul in Acts 23:8.

One of the things that atheists hold in common with the world's religions is persecution for their faith. Around the globe and throughout the ages, the espousal of nontheistic beliefs has frequently qualified as criminal behavior, even to the point of warranting capital punishment. Those nonbelievers who maintain that we must order our own lives rather than leaving the task to God and his anointed earthly governors are often seen as opposing the powers-that-be. To the degree that a religion controls government in any given place at any given time, nontheism is seen as a threat and a serious crime against public order.

The Christians were initially referred to as atheists, because their beliefs were wholly foreign, and the word is used often throughout history to denominate those who do not believe in the established religion. It was not an epithet to be taken lightly, and many a Christian in the early years of the Church paid with their lives for being so categorized. For all those believers who died for their faith and whose names fill up the *Lives of the Saints*, perhaps as many atheists also died as martyrs down through history, executed for nothing more than their nonbelief, hounded to death for not bending the knee, or tied to the stake and burned, or taken outside the town walls and stoned. In keeping with the ebb and flow of history and power, Christians went through a long period of dying for their faith, and then gradually converted into a religion whose believers executed others for the crime of nonbelief.

Apostasy and independent thinking are often perceived

by those in power as a threat to their position, something that needs to be eliminated or exiled from the community as rapidly as possible. To believers, atheism is a threat because it is what waits without the consolation of religion. For Christians in particular, in addition to the temptations of the flesh is the ever-present danger of doubt, the danger of an eroding belief in God and the divinity of Christ. Atheism, the conviction that God does not exist, is waiting, yawning like the very maws of hell, if the foundations of faith should crack. Faith is a bridge across a chasm of doubt. One of the Devil's favorite tools is doubt, he is always standing by waiting to whisper it into the ear of anyone who wavers. The voices of those who did not believe could lead others down the road to perdition, so they needed to be silenced.

The story of Hypatia of Alexandria is often cited as the moment in history when the death knell sounded for Greek rationalism and the reflective life and when the Dark Ages began. Hypatia was the daughter of Theon, an astronomer and mathematician of great note in Alexandria. She was born there around 370 CE, in that Mediterranean center of learning at the top of Egypt, and followed in her father's footsteps. She was a philosopher, mathematician, and inventor, a believer in the Greek gods, a Platonist rather than an atheist, an intellectual of high achievement, president for a time of the Alexandrian Academy. Cyril, the archbishop of Alexandria who would eventually be canonized, is said to have viewed Hypatia as a dangerous advocate of "paganism" and been jealous of her influence with Orestes, the city's prefect. Saint Cyril is thought to have been behind her murder in 415 CE by a mob that included many monks loyal to him.

Her death was recounted fifteen hundred years later in dramatic fashion by Mangusar Mugurditch Mangasarian, in a lecture given one evening to the Independent Religious Society of Chicago. Mangasarian was born in Turkey in 1859 and came to the United States to study for the Presbyterian ministry at Princeton. Some years afterward, he announced that he was leaving the ministry of his Philadelphia church in particular and the faith as a whole. He became a self-professed nonbeliever. In 1892, he was living in Chicago, where he led the local chapter of the American Ethical Culture Society. His retelling of Hypatia's story, quoted on Howard Landman's Web site about Hypatia, incorporated most of the errors and embellishments that have been added down through the centuries, but he got the basic facts right:

> Hypatia was a remarkably gifted woman. . . . Judging by the chronicles of the times, it appears that her beauty, which would have made even a Cleopatra jealous, was as great as her modesty, and both were matched by her eloquence, and all three surpassed by her learning.
>
> When Hypatia appeared in her chariot in front of her residence, suddenly five hundred men, all dressed

in black and cowled, five hundred monks, half-starved monks from the sands of the Egyptian desert—five hundred monks, soldiers of the cross—like a black hurricane, swooped down the street, boarded her chariot, and pulling her off her seat, dragged her by the hair of her head into a—how shall I say the word?—into a church! Some historians intimate that the monks asked her to kiss the cross, to become a Christian and join the nunnery, if she wished her life spared. At any rate, these monks under the leadership of St. Cyril's right-hand man, Peter the Reader, shamefully stripped her naked, and there, close to the altar and the cross, scraped her quivering flesh from her bones with oyster shells. . . . 'The mutilated body, upon which the murderers feasted their fanatic hate, was then flung into the flames.

Mangasarian's purple prose aside, Hypatia's murder at the hands of Christian monks is often cited as the event that marked the beginning of more than a thousand years of Church dominance. Her story has figured frequently in prose and poetry, appearing as early as 1736 in an essay by Voltaire, according to Maria Dzielska in her book, *Hypatia of Alexandria*. She describes Voltaire's take on the story. "She [Hypatia] was murdered, Voltaire asserts, because she believed in the Hellenic gods, the laws of rational Nature, and the capacities of the human mind free of imposed dogmas."

While the paganistic school continued for another couple of centuries in Alexandria after Hypatia's murder, until the Arabs invaded, the Church in Europe followed the example set by Saint Cyril's Alexandrian monks and often meted out some version of Hypatia's fate to nonbelievers. "The closing of the pagan philosophical schools by the Christian Emperor Justinian in 529 CE can be taken as marking the end of the Classical and freethinking period of thought," writes James Thrower in *Western Atheism: A Short History.*

During the Dark Ages that followed, Europe's Jews and atheists found themselves treated as one and the same in the eyes of ecclesiastical law. Both groups learned to keep their mouths shut, pledge loyalty to the God of the ruling Church, and keep any other thoughts they might have, or rituals they might perform, a secret. It was not until the late Middle Ages and the beginning of the Renaissance that Europeans began to feel once again "free of imposed dogmas" and at liberty not to believe in anything at all other than this world and the forces that turn it. The thousand years that passed between Hypatia's murder by monks and the Renaissance are a whole millennium from which no evidence of nonbelievers is found, yet reason tells us that they must have existed. Life was as arbitrary, brief and painful then as now, in fact more so. It is impossible to imagine that some people did not believe this is the only life we have. If so, they weren't writing about it.

The conflicts that the Church dealt with during those centuries did not frequently involve other faiths but were internecine in nature—internal squabbling, doctrinal here-sies, apostasies, ecumenical quibbling, excommunication. From the twelfth through the fifteenth centuries, the Inqui-sition developed into an all-powerful enforcer of the faith—four hundred long years of fear and dogma. The only record of atheism from that period is the Inquisition's list of those accused of unbelief who were tried for it and often died for it. It was a charge under which conversos were frequently prosecuted, those Jews who had converted to save their lives but who kept the Inquisitors in work. Conversos whose faith seemed insufficient were often charged with being unbelievers.

The Church's absolute dominion over the secular and the sacred began to give way in the late twelfth century, when the Arab and Jewish philosophers of the Mediterranean basin felt free enough to discuss out loud and publish some of the ideas that were revolutionizing their theological thinking. While the Jews were developing kabbalistic thought, Arab thinkers were translating from the Greek classics and writing commentaries on Aristotle. The writings of such Arabian theologians and philosophers as Ibn Sina (Avicenna) in the eleventh century and Ibn Rushd (Averroës) in the twelfth were dedicated to reconciling Aristotelian thinking with Islamic faith. They were only partially suc-cessful, but these works served the purpose of reintroducing Aristotle to European thinkers, along with certain of his ideas that were radical for the times, including the negation of personal immortality. The science of the Enlightenment would discard the Aristotelian concept of the world, but Aristotle's assertions were a starting point from which philosophical inquiry could begin advancing outside the boundaries delineated by the Church. The need for philosophers to cast a wider net was an implicit recognition that a wholly satisfactory explanation for the world and what happens when we die had yet to appear.

At the same time, science began to undergo tremendous changes. Through the Middle Ages, scientists had concentrated mostly on the elements, basing their research on Aristotle and studying alchemy. Medicine was practiced according to the doctrine that health depended on a balance of the four humors that affected people. Dissection was frowned upon by the Church, and tools for advancing medical knowledge were in short supply. The study of how the body was made and its method of functioning was severely discouraged.

While some of alchemy's presuppositions and theories were applied to the treatment of the ailing body, science was something well apart from medicine, dedicated to uncovering truths that were not necessarily of any utility to physicians. Although both disciplines were waging war against death, they were generally doing so with different strategies. The scientist was often ensconced in a university, while the physician's practice was a far more mechanical, hands-on job dealing with the unpleasant, odoriferous, and distasteful details of individual bodies.

The repair of the human body during the Dark Ages was

a brute profession, not a complex science. Physicians frequently worked as barbers in between doctoring, and the two jobs had a similar low status. By the time a physician was called to attend a sick person, there was frequently nothing to be done. Medicine was still largely based on the principles elaborated in the second century CE by Galen, a Greek physician. With bloodletting (phlebotomy) and diet being the two principal armaments available to doctors, it is no surprise they were held in low repute. In addition, the fact that they worked on the body, with all its negative connotations for believers—that gross, lustful, and untrustworthy sack of sloshing liquids—made medicine a less-than-desirable career choice for the educated aristocracy. In the Middle Ages, many of the physicians in Europe were Jews.

Science, medicine, and philosophy began to move closer together in the early part of the Renaissance, to form a base around which nonbelievers might group. The fifteenth and early sixteenth centuries were a remarkably fertile moment in history, and these years changed the course of European civilization. The age of exploration and colonization was beginning as Europeans made their way around the globe. At virtually the same time, Martin Luther was breaking with the Church to begin the Protestant Reformation, and Copernicus was declaring that the earth is not at the center of the universe, shortly followed by Galileo Galilei's explanation of the mechanics of Copernican theory. Galileo was condemned to prison for his heresy, but Church control was faltering, its vision of the world proving demonstrably insufficient.

Galileo may well have been grateful for the leniency of the sentence. His contemporary, Giordano Bruno, one of the few Europeans of his day courageous enough to support Copernican theory outspokenly, was not so lucky. He paid for his beliefs by being burned alive at the stake by the Inquisition, a nail driven through his tongue. Born near Naples in 1548, only five years after Copernicus died, he was ordained as a Dominican monk but was forced to flee Italy in 1576, when charges of heresy were brought against him. He spent the next fourteen years traveling around Europe developing his increasingly anticlerical philosophy, until he was lured back to Italy, where he was eventually denounced, imprisoned, and executed.

Italy was the ground where the seed of disbelief found fertile soil, or perhaps it was only that the Inquisition wanted to make an example on its home turf, but the Church and the Bible were no longer the last word on immortality. The 1500s saw a number of Italian atheists challenging accepted theology. An English traveler of 1551 was quoted by Nicholas Davidson in his essay "Atheism in Italy, 1500–1700" describing Italy as a place where "a man may freely discourse against what he will, against whom he lust: against any Prince, agaynst any, yea against God him selfe, and his whole religion."

A number of scholars and philosophers in sixteenth-century Italy made public their doubts about immortality and paid variously stiff penalties for doing so. As early as 1513, Pope Leo X issued a condemnation of anyone who taught that a soul dies with a person. The fact that he felt impelled to do so indicates that doubt had already breached the walls of Christian doctrine. Philosophers like Pietro Pomponazzi, Girolamo Cardano, and Andrea Cesalpino spent their lives in conflict with the ecclesiastical authorities.

The word *atheist* was used during the Middle Ages to describe anyone whose beliefs deviated from the norm, not simply those who were nontheists. David Wootton, in his article, "New Histories of Atheism," describes what was meant by the term. "This is not to say that these atheists would have denied the very existence of God. What we should study primarily are their arguments that concerned not the existence of God or his role in nature, but his relevance to human concerns for these are the arguments that contemporaries felt did most to undermine belief in the Christian God."

Inquisition records show that atheism was not confined to scientists, mathematicians, and philosophers. The Italian artisan class was literate they read and were aware of Aristotle and the classical writers. The Inquisition frequently charged merchants and artisans with various heresies. Speculation that immortality does not exist was not the exclusive property of a few philosophers and heretics but rather something that average people occasionally, and often to their great detriment, also espoused.

"In 1574," writes Nicholas Davidson, "the Venetian Inquisition received a denunciation against Commodo Canuove of Vicenza, in which he was accused of saying that 'we have never seen any dead man who has returned from the other world to tell us that paradise exists—or purgatory or hell; all these things are the fantasies of friars and priests, who wish to live without working and to pamper themselves with the goods of the Church.' "

Although the Inquisitors' records and charges are far from unimpeachable sources regarding the true beliefs of an accused, it is clear that doubt had entered the public discourse. Gerolamo Cardano, in the mid-sixteenth century, is said to have propounded fifty arguments against the immortality of the soul. He was a brilliant mathematician, physician, and inventor, accused of heresy in 1570 because he cast a horoscope for Jesus Christ.

Heretics and blasphemers were always at risk, and charges of atheism were not restricted to the highly educated. In 1601, a sixty-nine-year-old miller named Domenico Scandella, known as Menocchio, was burned at the stake by the Inquisition. He was from the Friuli region in northeastern Italy and was a prominent citizen there. He had served a term as mayor, and his milling business provided him a reliable income. Records from the time show that he spoke out frequently against the Church, its hierarchy, and its doctrine.

In 1583, Menocchio was denounced and charged with blasphemy and atheism but allowed to go free. He could not leave well enough alone, however, continuing to speculate out loud about the nature of God, insisting that Jesus was only a man, and disdaining the idea of a Resurrection to eternal heaven or hell. Menocchio was literate, and during his trials he made reference to a number of volumes ranging from the Bible to the Qur'an to the *Decameron*, according to Carlo Ginzburg in *The Worm and the Cheese*, an examination of the documents relating to Menocchio's case.

During the sixteenth and seventeenth centuries, heresy was a crime that sometimes carried a death sentence. In 1619, Guilio Cesare Vanini was found guilty of atheism by the Inquisition in Toulouse at the age of thirty-four. Born in Naples, he studied law at Padua and was ordained into the priesthood. However, he soon began expressing decidedly anticlerical opinions. "He led a roving life in France, Switzerland and the Low Countries, supporting himself by giving lessons and disseminating anti-religious views," according to the *Encyclopædia Britannica*. He had his tongue cut out and was strangled at the stake, then his body was cremated.

It was not until 1677 that the Catholic Church replaced execution with excommunication for those found guilty of atheism. As late as 1697, Protestants hung twenty-year-old Thomas Aikenhead for blasphemy in Edinburgh, Scotland, according to Michael Hunter's essay, "Aikenhead the Atheist." He was executed under a law that was passed by the Scottish Parliament in 1661, and which imposed the death penalty "for anyone who 'not being distracted in his wits Shall rail upon or curse God or any of the persons of the blessed Trinity.'

"A further act passed in 1695 both confirmed this and

also dealt with 'whoever hereafter shall in their writing or discourse, deny, impugn, or quarell, argue or reason, against the being of God, or any of the persons of the blessed Trinity, or the Authority of the Holy Scriptures of the Old and New Testaments, or the providence of God in the Government of the World.' "

By the end of the seventeenth century, things were changing, and executions for nonbelief were fewer. The tide was slowly turning. A belief in rational, scientific inquiry was spreading throughout Europe. The physical details of the world in which we live and of the bodies that each of us inhabits were understood to be more complex, remarkable, and important that previously realized.

"During this period it began to be borne more and more upon men's minds that this world was worthy of the attention of the best minds, and that man himself, irrespective of whatever supernatural affiliations he might be supposed to have, was not unworthy of study. The Renaissance marks the beginning of that secularized approach to the knowledge of man and his environment with which we today are so familiar," writes James Thrower.

People looked back to the Romans and the Greeks. They read and reread the Classical writers, and began to apply the principles they found there to their own lives—the humanist school was born. While the number of actual atheists—those who were willing to declare an absolute unbelief in any deity—in the early Renaissance was small, people once again began to have the freedom to imagine what they would of the nature of God and the afterlife. Science and reason began to impose themselves between the citizens and traditional Christian ideas about heaven and hell.

Philosophers are people who ponder professionally, but everyone practices philosophy in his or her own life. We all elaborate a lifetime of answers to questions such as: Why are we here? And what happens when we die? This is not just mental exercise and idle speculation, because the conclusions we reach individually will have a lot to do with not only how we live our own lives but also how we form our communities and behave toward one another. Once people began to believe that the earth was not at the center of the universe and to speculate that only oblivion waited after death, it changed the way they approached the world at hand.

At some point, people stopped looking backward to the Greeks and began looking forward to a time when they would understand why the world works as it does, and would adjust their lives accordingly. Increasingly, they looked to empirical science to provide answers. Advances like Galileo's invention of the microscope, medical discoveries such as Englishman William Harvey's of blood circulation controlled by the heart, and the writings of the French mathematician René Descartes contributed to an increasingly rationalistic worldview in which the concept of an afterlife was less important and eventually less credible. The Cartesian model, based on Descartes's perception of the human condition, formed the philosophical basis for the turn toward the future. While Descartes believed in God, he also believed in a universe that ran according to mathematical, rational principles governing the world and the living beings in it, an innovative approach to philosophy that laid the groundwork for the "modern" European thought that would follow and would eventually touch the lives of even the most modest citizens.

This turn toward a rationalism based on mathematical certainty and the repudiation of religious doctrine were not confined to Christians. One of the most influential thinkers of the seventeenth century was Baruch Spinoza, a Dutch Jew born in 1632, who studied Cartesianism as a young man and early on began to doubt Judaism. In late 1655 he stopped paying dues to the synagogue and showing up there for worship. The rabbis expelled him from the community in 1656, and they did so in a particularly definitive manner, according to Jonathan Israel's book *Radical Enlightenment*. "He was proscribed for no ordinary deviance, sacrilege, financial irregularity or heresy but open, sympathetic, premeditated, and blatant doctrinal rebellion of a fundamental kind that simply could not be ignored or smoothed over. . . . The elders ruled, with the rabbis' agreement, that the said Spinoza should be excommunicated and cast out from among the people of Israel."

This set Spinoza free to speak and publish his mind, and he did so for the next twenty-one years until his death. His was a system based on his early admiration for Cartesian thinking, constructed to explain and order the world by its natural properties. He believed the world could be apprehended by the human intellect and that this faculty would engender the correct way for people to live in that world. His work was widely known, and was translated in England, France, and Germany.

By the time Spinoza died in 1677, philosophers, scientists, physicians, and mathematicians were spending as much time disputing with each other as with the Church. Spinoza, for instance, did not accept the empirical scientific method initiated in his day by the English scientist, Robert Boyle. He believed, according to Israel, that experimental science could not be relied on to elaborate the basic framework of life, only its manifestations. Boyle, on the other hand, "considered the 'experimental way of philosophizing' the only secure basis for reliable knowledge, stressing the 'dimness and imperfections of our human understanding.'"

Despite their differences, they represented two parts of the ongoing revolution in philosophy and science. They shared a faith that the future would reveal life's whys and wherefores and that reason was capable of eventually explaining the mysteries of the human condition. While some saw this as blasphemy and warned that the wrath of God would be called down on the heads of nonbelievers, many found a new kind of hope in Rationalism, in the idea that human beings could take control of their lives and eventually create a world in which everything from plague to poverty could be controlled and eventually eradicated.

"From its origins in the 1650s and 1660s," writes Israel:

"the philosophical radicalism of the Early European Enlightenment characteristically combined immense reverence for science, and for mathematical logic, along with some form of non-providential deism, if not outright materialism and atheism along with unmistakably republican, even democratic tendencies."

The spirit of the times was not slow in crossing from the Continent to the British Isles. As early as 1617, the Spanish ambassador to England estimated that there were 90,000 atheists in the country, according to Keith Thomas in *Religion and the Decline of Magic*. He also notes that Sir Walter Raleigh was said to belong to a group who denied that an afterlife existed and subscribed to a belief that oblivion waits when we die.

Actual unbelievers remained few, perhaps due to the severe penalties that could be meted out for the crimes of heresy, blasphemy, and atheism, or perhaps because in the seventeenth century, a world totally devoid of God was too frightening to contemplate with empirical science still in its infancy. Martin Fotherby, dean of Canterbury, wrote a book in 1622 refuting atheism while at the same time admitting that few strict atheists existed. He is quoted in an essay by G. E. Aylmer: "To what end this whole worke serveth, which is written against Atheists, if they be few, or none such? . . . Yet there be very many, that beleeue [believe] it weakly: and that being overcome by sodaine [sudden] passions and temptations do often doubt, and distrust; whether there be any God? . . . And few men can escape the very same temptations. Therefore, of this sort of Atheists, there is as great a plenty, as of the first sort, a scarcity."

Thomas Hobbes, who died in 1679 at the advanced age of ninety-one, was a believer, but with a naturalistic and materialistic view of God and the world that differed substantially from the Christian doctrine of his day. While he always attempted to integrate his thinking into a Christian context, his work was viewed with suspicion by the authorities, and one year, when plague and fire decimated London's population, a parliamentary committee was formed to investigate Hobbes's thinking as set forth in his major work, *Leviathan*. Lawmakers speculated that God could be punishing London for Hobbes's impiety, according to Thrower's *Western Atheism*.

Nevertheless, in the British Isles as in the rest of Europe, medicine and science joined hands with philosophy in a relentless march toward Rationalism. By the early eighteenth century, atheistic writings had appeared in German, Dutch, French, Italian, and English. By midcentury, David Hume was publishing in England, Baron d'Holbach and Jacques-André Naigeon in France, Holland had a number of Spinozist philosophers elaborating on the late master's system, and many German intellectuals were warmly receptive to all of these.

Atheism also appeared in the New World in the late eighteenth century, most notably in the work of the Englishman Thomas Paine, who arrived in North America in 1774. He was perhaps more what is called a deist—someone who believes that God set the world in motion and stepped away, uninvolved with the outcome, knowable only by the great work left behind: our world and our innate sense of right and wrong. Paine had many readers—his pre–Revolutionary War book, *Common Sense*, sold some 500,000 copies in the mid-1770s, according to Susan Jacoby in her book *Freethinkers*. What Paine did to shock his readers in 1794, when he published *The Age of Reason*, was to rank Christianity as just another pernicious myth invented to control believers. His attack on Christianity and the Bible gained him the epithet of atheist from many of his fiercest critics.

"The most detestable wickedness, the most horrid cruelties, and the greatest miseries, that have afflicted the human race have had their origin in this thing called revelation, or revealed religion," wrote Paine. "It has been the most dishonourable belief against the character of the divinity, the most destructive to morality, and the peace and happiness of man, that ever was propogated since man began to exist."

The reign of humans and the Age of Reason were beginning, the dominion of God over the world was ending. A wall was erected between government and organized religion that was intended to be unbreachable. The American Revolution not only emancipated the nation from the rule of England but also guaranteed that people could believe what they wanted, including nothing at all. Legislation and government were to remain wholly independent from religion.

Paine, who had been a favorite in North America when he published his revolutionary writings, fell into disrepute when he refused to tone down his attacks on organized religion. He went to France, where he was jailed by the Jacobins. When released, he returned to the United States where there was considerable popular sentiment against letting him stay, but his close friend Thomas Jefferson had just been elected president, and he granted Paine asylum in 1802. Seven years later, Paine died at the age of seventy-two. He spent his last years as a guest in the house of James Madison, who would follow Jefferson as president, taking office in 1809, the same year Paine died. Madison, along with Jefferson and Adams, was one of the early Republic's most influential voices for a wholly secular Constitution.

Jefferson, the architect of democracy, was no less a critic of Christianity than Paine. In a letter to John Adams, the second president of the nation and a close friend (they both died on July 4, 1826), he wrote, "The truth is, that the greatest enemies of the doctrine of Jesus are those, calling themselves the expositors of them, who have perverted them to the structure of a system of fancy absolutely incomprehensible, and without any foundation in his genuine words. And the day will come, when the mystical generation of Jesus, by the Supreme Being as his father, in the womb of a virgin, will be classed with the fable of the generation of Minerva in the brain of Jupiter."

In another letter, Jefferson wrote: "I have recently been examining all the known superstitions of the world, and do not find in our particular superstition [Christianity] one redeeming feature. They are all alike founded on fables and mythology."

It is no accident that the word *God* does not appear in the United States Constitution, as Susan Jacoby points out in her book *Freethinkers*. The nation was founded on secular principles. People believed that religion could have many proper spheres of influence in personal and community life but that government should not be one of them. It is painful in the early twenty-first century, when the United States is as close to being a fundamentalist Christian theocracy as it has ever come, to read what the founding fathers wrote about the importance of maintaining a strict separation between church and state.

By the end of the eighteenth century, across Europe and in North America, the democratic experiment was beginning, and voices of nonbelief were audible. Although the first of many fundamentalist Christian renaissances in the United States began at the start of the nineteenth century, a steady stream of women and men raised their voices to proclaim their disbelief throughout the 1800s. All this rejection of Church authority and doubt of Church doctrine on both sides of the Atlantic happened even before Charles Darwin proclaimed his theory of evolution. In 1859, the publication of *The Origin of the Species* provided an empirically sound explanation for the way in which life developed. Humanists and atheists finally had a scientific framework on which to construct their beliefs.

"Did an infinite God create the children of men?" asked Robert Ingersoll, known as "the Great Agnostic," in his last public address, delivered to the American Free Religious Association in Boston on June 2, 1899. "Why did he create the intellectually inferior? Why did he create the deformed and helpless? Why did he create the criminal, the idiotic, the insane?"

With Darwin's theory at last came an explanation in concrete terms for why the world *is*, and why it is like it is. "For freethinkers like Ingersoll," writes Jacoby, "Darwinian evolution offered an unambiguous opportunity to explain in natural terms what had, for eons, been explained solely in supernatural terms."

Ingersoll, who died in 1899 at the age of sixty-six, was the nation's preeminent orator and freethinker. The son of a Presbyterian minister from upstate New York, he was raised mostly in Illinois. He served as a Union officer during the Civil War and had a brief career in politics, but his outspoken agnosticism meant that his political prospects were dim to nonexistent. While the public might not have voted for him, they were glad to turn out and listen to him speak, something he did to soldout crowds in cities and towns across the nation.

In an 1877 lecture, quoted by Jacoby, Ingersoll said, "I would rather belong to that race that commenced a skullless vertebrate and produced Shakespeare, a race that has before it an infinite future, with the angel of progress beckoning forward, upward and onward forever—I had rather belong to such a race, commencing there, producing this, and with that hope, than to have sprung from a perfect pair upon which the Lord has lost money every moment from that day to this."

In the aftermath of World War I, it is generally agreed that in the United States the pendulum swung back, and that fundamentalist Christianity enjoyed a resurgence in both believers and influence. The country took a conservative tack, which was reversed only because of the Great Depression. Darwin's theory has always been a lightning rod in the struggle between religious conservatives and advocates of a purely secular government—no less in Dayton, Tennessee, in the 1925 trial of John Scopes for teaching evolution in a public high school, than in the movement eighty years later to have evolution removed from the biology classroom, or at least to teach from textbooks that allot equal space to Darwin's theory and the evangelically inspired "intelligent design" concept of creation.

In short, the struggle goes on. Darwin's nineteenth-century theory of evolution and Watson and Crick's first revelations about genes and DNA in the twentieth century meant that by the year 2000, scientific evidence had continued to accumulate, that seemed to favor a mechanistic explanation for life and what happens after death. However, an increasingly vocal and politically astute group of fundamentalist Christians gave no quarter to science and struggled against secularization on many fronts. For forty-five years, the Cold War reproduced the battle in political terms, and once the communist atheists were vanquished, the infidel Muslim terrorists appeared to take their place, waiting to overrun the United States and turn Christians into martyrs.

With the disintegration of the Soviet Union and the conversion of China into the largest producer of consumer goods in the world, Christian America was left as the world's only superpower. Atheism as a national faith had failed to prosper. Doubt, however, like death, affects Christians and communists alike. The case is far from closed. Communism may have virtually disappeared and the "good life" may be the gold standard, but plenty of people still conclude that the salient feature of living is that we are alive only once. Now and nevermore. Those who choose to voice that opinion are still at some risk around the globe, although the degree of risk varies greatly. In the United States, a label of atheist is enough to destroy a political career but it is not yet a criminal offense. In the year 2006, it's easier to imagine a Jewish woman as president of the United States than a professed atheist. It could be worse— in Iran, talking about atheism around the neighborhood is still enough to land a person in jail.

In Spain, less than a lifetime ago, that was also the case. While no specific law against atheism existed, there were laws about offending public order and decency broad enough to warrant arresting left-wingers, homosexuals, and atheists alike. Any, such as there were, kept their mouths shut in public, as they had learned to do in Spain during most of the years since the Middle Ages.

Francisco Franco died in 1975, but the succeeding governments, both socialist and conservative, continued to provide the Church with tax exemptions, subsidies, and a variety of special treatments. Church attendance fell off rapidly after a secular, democratic government was installed, and surveys consistently put the number of Spaniards who define themselves as "unreligious" at about 17 percent of the population, but it was not until 1994 that the first Spanish association of atheists was formed in Barcelona. Even then, a number of his friends told founder Albert Riba that it was a risky thing to do. Riba has a civil service job, working in the social security administration, he told me, and has never had to worry about losing his job for speaking his mind. "The first time I went on television and said I was an atheist, in 1994, all my friends asked how I could be so brave as to say in public that I was an atheist? Some of them would have lost their jobs, or at least harmed their careers by doing that."

Riba, fifty-eight, has a big frame and a large girth, white hair that he keeps short and combed, a trim, gray beard and mustache. He wears steel-rimmed glasses and laughingly confessed, when I spoke with him in 2005, that he talks more and faster than anyone he knows. "Our group, the Association of Atheists in Catalonia, is still the only one in Spain. We began with four people. It was like a desert here for atheists. We began by publishing small magazines and bulletins every few months. We elaborated an ideological base and gained in numbers up to about six hundred people, and by the year 2000 we were recognized as a legitimate social force. We established relations with the administrations of Catalonia in Barcelona and the government in Madrid. Atheists, both in the law and in reality, must have exactly the same rights as all other citizens."

In other places in the world less tolerant than the United States or Spain, a charge of atheism can still mean imprisonment or even execution. Science and religion continue to struggle, and after thousands of years, neither one can prove whether any part of us does or does not survive death. All we know is that our lives seem terrifyingly short, packed full of love and suffering, tenderness and terror, and we cannot, with complete assurance say why.

La Infinitat de la Tendresa (*The Infinity of Tenderness*), digital composition by Victòria Rabal, 1999. Courtesy of the artist.

Over and Out

A man hath no preeminence above a beast: for all is vanity. All go into one place; all are of the dust, and all turn to dust again.

Ecclesiastes 3:19–20

For many people, the theory of evolution effectively delivered the *coup de grace* to the religious view of history. The idea that our lives and the larger world were unfolding according to God's plan, which gave us dominion over all living things, was no longer tenable. The place that humans occupied in the world and our relationship to the rest of the species living in it were forever changed by the concept of evolution. It was, after all, only two hundred years ago that educated people believed the earth was six thousand years old and at the center of the universe, as Francis Crick reminds readers in his book, *The Astonishing Hypothesis: The Scientific Search for the Soul.*

"We now know that all living things, from bacteria to ourselves, are closely related at the biochemical level," writes Crick, the British biochemist and physicist who shared a Nobel Prize with James Watson in 1962 for their discovery of the molecular structure of DNA. "We know that life has existed on earth for billions of years, and that the many species of plants and animals have changed, often radically, over that time. The dinosaurs have gone and in their place many new species of mammals have arisen. We can watch the basic processes of evolution happening today, both in the field and in our test tubes."

Over the course of the past five hundred years, the idea of the relative importance of people to the rest of creation has diminished drastically. A world with a divinely imposed order in which human beings are at the center no longer seems likely. What seems more probable is a world with an order and structure based on something much closer to Democritus's atomic system than Saint Paul's revelations on the road to Damascus. This shift in our notion of the world has radically changed the concept of how humans think. "A modern neurobiologist sees no need for the religious concept of a soul to explain the behavior of humans and other animals," writes Crick. "One is reminded of the question Napoleon asked after Pierre-Simon Laplace had explained to him the workings of the solar system: 'Where does God come into all this?' To which Laplace replied: 'Sire, I have no need of that hypothesis.' "

Science cannot yet explain all of the world's mysteries, but many of its best practitioners are convinced they are on the right road to doing so. They are certain that the explanation of how our bodies and our world function is mechanistic, an entirely biochemical process, which we are capable of one day wholly understanding. Most good scientists will explain that they do not personally hope to make a great discovery but what they want to do when they get up to go to work each morning is to find small, true things to add to the overall web of small true things, which in turn form a pattern of large true things that we can know with certainty about the world. Scientists dedicate their lives to uncovering their own particles of truth in the belief that eventually the whole will be revealed.

In the millennia-old opposition of theists and nontheists, belief seems to have shifted over the past couple of centuries, slowly but surely, towards the nontheists. The scientific discoveries of the past few hundred years and our understanding of how life functions argue for a world in which neither divinity nor immortality exist. The longer time goes on without Christ coming back to end it for eternity, the less possible seems the Parousia, the second and final coming. Ditto for the Jewish messiah. The Muslim paradise sounds more and more like fiction, and even granting that reincarnation might exist, if we do not carry memories from one life to the next, what's the difference?

As science gains credence through an ongoing revelation of empirically proven processes, more and more people are convinced that it offers the most reasonable and attractive explanation for how and why things happen as they do. The mechanistic approach to life is, however, not a vision of things that lends itself easily to the idea of immortality. Belief in an afterlife of any sort among scientists is not widespread. In a 1914 survey cited by Corliss Lamont in his book *The Illusion of Immortality*, only 36.9 percent of "eminent" U.S. scientists believed in an afterlife. That was just at the beginning of World War I. Instead of "the war to end all wars," it proved to be only the beginning of the slaughter. The century ahead would unfold in a dark, bloody, and discouraging history, while simultaneously, huge scientific steps were made toward understanding life's basic components.

Lamont himself wrote in 1934, "All science is based ultimately on probabilities. And in this case the probabilities against the human personality surviving in any worth-while way the event called death seem to me so overwhelming that we are justified in regarding immortality as an illusion."

In 1997, another survey of biologists, physicists, and

mathematicians, all members of the U.S. National Academy of Sciences, found fewer than 10 percent who said they believed in God, according to Cornelia Dean, writing in the *New York Times.* It is highly possible that if we ever do perceive the whole and how it works, it will become crystal clear that oblivion is our postdeath fate. Most scientists evidently think so. However, they temper their judgments with mercy, and most are also convinced that this bleak prognosis for the end of life will be offset by the fact that the same body of knowledge that informs us of our unenviable fate will also enable us to prolong and improve this life to a great degree, as we learn more about the basic components of our bodies and our minds. Perhaps we shall finally fashion a world at peace, in which successive generations all have at least enough to live while they are alive: food, clean water, shelter, health care, and an education. Perhaps we shall come to view ours as the best of all possible worlds, given the undeniable reality of death—a world in which that inevitable personal extinction is greatly delayed by things such as stem cells grown to create replacements as our original bodies age and get ill or weak, or in which we learn how to turn off the "death gene."

Juan Valcárcel thinks it may be possible. "The goal of science is not to defeat death or give us better health," he told me in his small office down one of a number of identical corridors at the Catalan Institute for Research and Advanced Studies, part of a new biogenetic research park being built in Barcelona, beside the Mediterranean. "The goal is pure understanding. However, we are living beings under certain rules that are written in the genes and the way genes interact with our environment. It is not at all inconceivable that we shall be able to understand the process of aging to a point where we shall be able to slow it down extensively or even prevent it. That's a very nice consequence of knowledge and trying to understand the world."

Valcárcel is forty-three years old, born in Lugo, a small Galician city on the northwest coast of Spain. He arrived in Barcelona in 2002 via a research stint at the University of Massachusetts and another in Heidelberg, Germany, and directs a research team investigating gene expression. He is a lean, intense man with a ready smile, clean-shaven with graying hair cut short. "A human being is driven by a number of sophisticated, complicated laws, some of which we can't yet imagine. But what we are is written in terms of molecules, and we are no different from other systems."

The Catalan government has made it clear how it stands on the question of Church versus science. The Catholic Church in Catalonia still receives various tax breaks and subsidies from the Catalan government, a vestige of the Franco dictatorship, but the percentage of the overall budget this represents has been steadily declining. Expenditures on the research and development sector, however, have grown drastically. Bureaucrats have developed a strategy to attract research facilities, which include the project down by the sea. Beside the office building where Valcárcel works is a striking new seaside building described by its builders, when they announced the project in the newspapers, as "the Cathedral of the park," the design of which is based on the form of a protein. The park is envisioned as a research campus where university scientists and biomedical businesses will coexist in easy reach of one another.

Barcelona is a city that is endlessly remaking itself—from a drab industrial city in the 1980s to the upbeat, hip, post-Olympics tourist destination of the 1990s. The repositioning of the Catalan capital as a research center for the twenty-first century is wholly in character. The building where Valcárcel has his office is like something out of a science fiction film, with a warren of hallways each lined with small, brightly lit offices occupied by scientists and computers, each office affiliated with a lab space somewhere else in the edifice; one long glass wall looks out to the beach and the sea. It is a far cry from many of the gray research installations in cold northern Europe, and it is not hard to imagine why a scientist might see it as a more congenial place to work than Germany or England or France.

Juan Valcárcel's personal trajectory is a lot like that of the Catalan government. He began as a believing Catholic who invested a lot of energy in his beliefs but gradually became convinced that he needed to look to science for his answers. Growing up in Galicia, he was given a Catholic education by the Franciscans. "I owe a lot of who I am to that education," he said. "They insisted a lot on the idea that we should consider our lives like projects for which we are responsible. They encouraged us to think about what our life was worth not in terms of money but of other people. For them, there was no problem in reconciling religion and evolution. God put a cell in the sea and evolution could be the plan of God and is a perfectly valid approach.

"The main problem for me with religion is that it invokes faith, which means that there is something beyond your capacity to think and that you have to believe it, if you want to live forever. Religion is not evolving. The Church has basically the same concepts and ideas it has had for thousands of years. A believer has no alternative but to accept it. With equations you can revise and change, and it seems much more interesting than just giving up your brain. I absolutely believe we can find a mechanistic explanation for everything, including things like consciousness that are still mysteries today."

Consciousness. It is one of the things that scientists have yet to explain satisfactorily—how it functions and what a mind consists of—yet many of the world's outstanding scientists share Valcárcel's conviction of the basic mechanistic explanation that mind and matter are one self-contained unit, biochemically generated and biochemically obliterated. People become who they do because of multiple factors, things like childhood experiences and environmental pollution, but all of these influences are mediated biologically and chemically.

Nevertheless, science still has a long row to hoe before demonstrating empirically that this is the case. No one can yet provide a coherent explanation for the detailed awareness of the world that each of us has—what we see, hear, feel, and imagine. Can cellular signals and chemical releases really determine why it is that I perceive colors or hear tones and react emotionally to them, things that are in reality nothing more than wavelengths? Is my chemical conditioning so strong that a wholly imaginary erotic thought can raise my penis? How can a book or a film or a piece of music move me to tears? How does memory work, where is it stored, and what is the process I use to retrieve it?

For millennia, the soul was the place where consciousness was believed to dwell. The soul was thought to be the seat of the mind, this curious mental part of us, our minds apparently unique among all the species in the curious and distinguishing human capacity for reflective thought and feeling. This self-awareness that we have inside our heads, this inexplicable capacity for reason inside each of us, the "still small voice" of conscience, our depths, and the subtleties of our emotions are all components of ourselves that have long been thought to prove the existence of an individual soul.

In an essay published in 1929, "The Possibility of Survival from a Scientific Point of View," the scientist Sir Oliver Lodge wrote:

> It has become pretty obvious that human nature is more than mechanism, that it utilizes the physical energy and the physical and chemical processes of its

organism, but that in every important aspect it transcends those processes. Even the mere sensation of color and tone are more than belong to the physical world: physically there is nothing except vibrations of different frequency. . . . These higher attributes are displayed and manifested by chemical processes, but in themselves they transcend and outlast them; they belong to another order of existence, interpenetrating and utilizing the material, but not limited by or coextensive with it.

It may have seemed "pretty obvious" to Lodge, but in addition to being a well-known English scientist, he was a spiritist and a founding member of the British Society for Psychic Research. Science apart, he was convinced of another plane of existence waiting just beyond this one. His convictions about the limited applicability of the mechanistic approach were, and remain, very much a minority view. Most "eminent" scientists believe that the process of consciousness will eventually be deciphered and integrated into an entirely mechanistic view of human life. They also concede that science is still a long way away from that goal.

That is the scientific challenge that drew Francis Crick, after his codiscovery of DNA. In order to approach the mystery of consciousness, he decided to explore the neurobiology of vision to investigate how we see—both the process by which the retina communicates an image to the brain and how the brain then models and acts on that image. It is something that our brains are doing every moment we have our eyes open. Crick and his colleague, Christof Koch, began with the conviction that consciousness is an entirely neuronal process and that visual consciousness is mappable. By identifying exactly how vision worked in the brain, they hoped to understand how consciousness manifests itself. They hypothesized that neuronal activity was always associated with consciousness and that by locating and investigating what they called the "neuronal correlates of consciousness," they could begin to decipher how it worked.

For most of the last few centuries and with few exceptions, brain research was carried out with strictly physiological goals. Researchers like Pierre Broca and Karl Wernicke in the mid-nineteenth century and Walter Penfield in the early twentieth located specific areas of the brain that controlled different functions. Once it was understood that different minute sections of the brain were dedicated to various tasks, the research goal was to map it, primarily for use when something went wrong. With a map of the brain's functions, repairs were much easier to attempt. Investigation of things like thought, memory, and consciousness were all largely ignored in favor of research that could serve medicine. In *The Astonishing Hypothesis*, Crick wrote, "Looked at in the perspective of human history, the main object of scientific research on the brain is not merely to understand and cure various medical conditions, important though this task may be, but to grasp the true nature of the human soul. Whether this term is metaphorical or literal is exactly what we are trying to discover."

Like Freud, he was under no illusion about how difficult his ideas would prove for the general public to accept. It was not enough to question doctrine or even the existence of a deity. Modern man had to dig deep and change the underlying ways in which we have thought about the soul over the centuries, and this is harder to do than simply proclaiming disbelief. Crick wrote:

> Many educated people, especially in the Western world, also share the belief that the soul is a metaphor and that there is no personal life either before conception or after death. They may call themselves atheists, agnostics, humanists or just lapsed believers, but they all deny the claims of major religions. Yet this does not mean they normally think of themselves in a radically different way. The old habits of thought die hard. A man may, in religious terms, be an unbeliever but psychologically he may continue to think of himself in much the same way as a believer does, at least for everyday matters.
>
> We need, therefore, to state the idea in stronger terms. The scientific belief is that our minds—the behavior of our brains—can be explained by the interactions of nerve cells (and other cells) and the molecules associated with them. This is to most people a really surprising concept. It does not come easily to

believe that I am the detailed behavior of a set of nerve cells, however many there may be and however intricate their interactions.

To demonstrate that consciousness is an entirely physical process might not constitute sure and certain proof that nothing waits for us after death, but for nonbelievers it would amount to strong evidence that even the most mysterious parts of our human selves are explicable as biochemical processes. Crick certainly thought so. In June 2003, ill with the cancer that would take his life eighteen months later at the age of eighty-eight, he told Margaret Wertheim in an interview published in the *New York Times*, "In the fullness of time, educated people will believe there is no soul independent of the body, and hence no life after death."

That Crick and Koch chose vision as the means to investigate their "astonishing hypothesis" is not surprising. Whatever mechanisms are involved in human consciousness can surely be found at work in the process of how we see things. Sight is the most complex and remarkable of our senses. Vision, optics, and the eye have fascinated physicians and philosophers since the earliest times. Many of the Greeks, including Plato, Euclid, Aristotle, Democritus, and Epicurus, theorized about vision, as did the thinkers who built on their work down through the centuries. Until the mid-1800s, the study of vision and optics was primarily done with the same sense—sight—that was being studied, because observation was the primary tool at hand. That is a situation not unlike the one faced by Crick and Koch and the others who study consciousness and how the mind works, a problem that is approached with the mind itself. It is a daunting task.

"The forebrain is a highly connected and fiendishly complex tapestry of neuronal networks," writes Christof Koch in his book *The Quest for Consciousness: A Neurobiologial Approach.* "Fiendishly complex" is just right and getting more so all the time. However, the complexity of the task does not dissuade or discourage scientists like Koch. The aim of his and Crick's research, he writes, is nothing less than to explain "all aspects of the first-person perspective of consciousness." The task will require simultaneous tracking of consciousness, behavior and neuronal events in an individual. "It will not be easy," Koch admits, "but then no truly worthwhile task ever is.

"We live at a unique point in the history of science. The technology to discover and characterize how the subjective mind emerges out of the objective brain is within reach. The next years will prove decisive."

What is at stake is nothing less than proving that human life is a closed system, requiring nothing of the divine for its functioning. If the process giving rise to consciousness can be discovered, it will be a huge step forward in the evolution of scientific understanding. "If such a theory can be formulated—a big if—without resorting to new ontological entities that can't be objectively defined and measured, then the scientific endeavor, dating back to the Renaissance, will have risen to its last great challenge," writes Koch. "Humanity will have a closed-form, quantitative account of how mind arises out of matter. This is bound to have significant consequences for ethics, including a new conception of humans that might radically contradict the traditional images that men and women have made of themselves through the ages and cultures."

Where Crick and Koch use vision to locate the neural activity of consciousness, another group of researchers looks to memory as the process that holds the key. How does memory work? No one knows. Names have appeared for parts of the process: each discrete memory, for instance, is called an engram. One current school of thought holds that the process is driven by the laws of quantum physics. Two Japanese scientists, Mari Jibu, a brain scientist, and a theoretical physicist, Kunio Yasue, have collaborated in a theory of consciousness, which they write about in their book *Quantum Brain Dynamics and Consciousness: An Introduction*. For those without multiple doctorates in physics, mathematics, and biochemistry, the book is slow going, but their assertions about how the brain works make for fascinating reading.

Consciousness is such a complicated process, in fact, that one school of thought holds that the brain can never know itself, convinced the way in which consciousness works is beyond the capacity of the human mind to understand. The British philosopher Colin McGinn posited in 1999 that humans cannot understand their own consciousness because we lack the capacity to do so. Our minds are simply not designed for the task they are "cognitively closed" to the possibility of understanding their own workings. It is as if a dog was to try and learn mathematics—its brain is simply not up to it. So, argues McGinn, the workings of our minds are forever inaccessible to us.

Scientists generally do not agree. They are no more willing to accept the hypothesis that consciousness is outside their capacity to understand than they are willing to accept that threescore and ten years is our divinely appointed life span and that beyond this we have no chance to fend off death other than good genes and a lot of luck. Most researchers are convinced that the length of our lives is open-ended and that science will continue to push back the inevitable. However, the inescapable truth is that we are not built to last forever. Even if a time arrives when we are able to replace failing parts and doctors have warehouses of spare body parts from the smallest to the largest at their disposal for those who can afford to buy them, it is impossible to imagine that our physical parts can be replaced indefinitely. Tissues, joints, veins, lungs, lights, and livers all age. The human being is designed to wear out. No one has ever proven that death is not our individual lot. So many billions born and died, and not a single one has escaped it.

It is a fate we share with the animal world. Some people say *Homo sapiens* is the only species that knows its time is limited and death waits. This notion may be no more than human hubris. Animals know when they're hungry, thirsty, tired, threatened, or loved, and it seems likely that somewhere programmed in their cells is a sense of an allotted span, the need to protect and nurture what lives while it lives.

Our lack of knowledge about what constitutes our own consciousness is matched by our ignorance about what it is like to be an animal. It seems fairly safe to conclude that animals lack the reflective consciousness to contemplate their own mortality or even, perhaps, to imagine themselves from without, rather than simply to act from within. However, we cannot say for sure that any of these things are the case. We cannot even declare for certain how much pain an animal feels, or whether it suffers pain in the same way we do, much less whether it feels sorrow.

Numerous researchers apply McGinn's assertion about human consciousness to that of animals and declare it a waste of time to investigate whether animals have a consciousness, because we are missing the necessary tools to arrive at a definitive answer. The lack of a common language between species makes it impossible. Since an animal can never tell us what it is thinking, if it is thinking anything at all, our conclusions will always be speculative and unprovable. The perception of animal consciousness studies as a waste of time was strongly reinforced during much of the twentieth century by the almost complete dominion of behaviorism in the field of animal psychology, which held that external influences and learned experience were the only forces at play in determining how an animal acted and reacted. Funding for animal consciousness studies in the field of animal behavior was not available. Behaviorism was what professors taught, or they did not teach at all.

It is frequently said that animals may know something, but they do not know that they know it. It is simply there. Nevertheless, many species do display a wide range of individual behaviors. Like ourselves, they have rich communication between members of their communities, they can distinguish between individuals, and they a capacity to adapt, to imagine, and to plan for a future. Behaviorism in animal psychology has waned, and increasing numbers of researchers posit the possibility that animals do have a consciousness, different from ours, obviously, but including many of the same elements, possibly including thought. How could it be otherwise, they ask, when we share so much of our genetic structure with the animal kingdom, when we are virtually identical to our simian cousins in the way we are constructed?

Those supporting something other than behaviorist interpretations of animal mental processes frequently point to the work of Donald Griffin, a member of the National Academy of Sciences and a professor for many years at Harvard, who assailed the behaviorists in the early 1990s. He drew together experimental data from many animal studies—from fieldwork and experimental evidence—to make a reasonable case for animal consciousness. His work opened up the field of animal behavior to other kinds of hypotheses than simply instinct-based cognition.

Observers have written that elephants do seem to have a conscious sense of what death is and a conscious response to it. The animals are said to gather together the bones of dead elephants that have been scattered and occasionally to cover a dead body with vegetation or stand around it silently for a long period of time. Some simians also seem to mourn family members when they die. "Chimpanzees feel profound emotions," said Jordi Sabater i Pi. "For instance, they are greatly affected by the death of others in their family. They grieve. They are sad."

Do animals think about death? Sabater i Pi, now eighty-two and a self-described agnostic, lives in his flat with his wife in a working-class Barcelona neighborhood. He spent thirty years in the jungles of Equatorial Guinea and western Africa, observing gorillas, chimpanzees, and bonobos, Homo sapiens's closest relatives. Humans share about 99 percent of their genome with bonobos. Sabater i Pi's most important discovery was that chimpanzees took sticks and broke off the twigs and made a tool that could be used to dig up termites to eat out of their nests. It was evidence of a far more sophisticated thought process than previously ascribed to chimps and was a fundamental observation in a radical rethinking of animal psychology.

Sabater i Pi also collaborated with Dian Fossey in her work with mountain gorillas and coauthored a paper with her. He is a naturalist of a high order, the sort who makes his own drawings of what he sees, even when accompanied in his fieldwork by a photographer. The walls of his study are lined with his detailed renderings of the animals he has observed: an African gray parrot, a frog, a gorilla.

Does a simian know it is going to die? "I don't know," said Sabater i Pi. "I just don't know, but it could be. It certainly could be. Many different kinds of animals react strongly to death. It's possible chimpanzees know they're going to die."

Who knows if animals think about death? What it is like to be an animal? No one knows, yet. Our understanding of the world is far from over. Our own consciousness, which has grown apart from the bonobo's in only the past few million years, is something that we cannot yet describe, much less control. On we go, spiraling through generations of war, rape, genocide, the same bloody horrors generation after generation. The monotheistic faithful, responsible for much of the slaughter, are wont to hold that without a belief in God the world would fall apart—humans would revert to an "animal" state, living only for their own self-interest during their own brief lives. Not so, respond the atheists, who insist that an ethical code exists for those who believe that this life is all we have and who feel an imperative to make *this* world better.

Belief or nonbelief does not have anything to do with whether people live moral lives, treating others as they would wish to be treated. For all the nonbelievers like Hitler or Stalin or Pol Pot who held human life so cheaply, there were plenty who did their bloody work proclaiming that God wanted it thus. The fact is that evil arises in believers and nonbelievers, alike. Where it does *not* arise is in animals, said Jordi Sabater i Pi, leaning forward across the table in his living room to remind me in a low, intense voice that evil and greed are human qualities.

"This kind of evil is not in animals," he said with all the conviction of someone who has spent eighty years in both jungles and cities. "Animals do fight over territory and domination, but they don't have the kind of cerebral evil that exists, that has always, *always* existed in humans. Its roots are anthropocentric. Most people think they have nothing in common with animals they are absolutely unwilling to admit that animals have the same rights as we do. They are wrong."

If it is so on earth, it must surely be so in heaven. So say believers from Nashville to Vanarasi. Everything dies. It is the fate of all animals and human beings we share the same inevitable cessation of life. If salvation exists for humans, must it not exist also for animals? Jon Roebuck, pastor of Nashville's Woodmont Baptist Church, hopes so. He wrote me: "I own a small Maltese dog that loves me in spite of myself, who always offers me the same affection and love each time I come into his presence. . . . Because of the love I have for my own pet, I want to think that the animal world is in some mysterious way caught up in the forever Kingdom of God. I do not however, know of any Scripture that supports or denies such a claim."

In Vanarasi, even a mosquito, even a fly is saved from further rebirth by dying in Kashi. When people die, Lord Shiva is said to whisper the dharma mantra into his or her right ear at the moment of death. This mantra brings the person understanding and sets his or her soul free to return from whence it came. Sanjay Sahi, who had spent his whole life in Varanasi, told me he had some information about this that he wanted me to know. He owned a guest house along the river by Asi ghat where he lived with his wife in one room behind the reception desk. He constantly chewed betel, and his teeth were worn down to red nubs.

"That this happens, Shiva whispering into the right ear, is scientifically proven," he said. "Lots of people here have heard of this—there was an experiment where scientists here packed mosquitos in cotton, packed them in so they couldn't turn, couldn't move at all. Then they let them die. And the head always turned toward the left, always turned, so Shiva could whisper the dharma mantra in its right ear. It has also been proven that this does not happen elsewhere, only in Kashi."

What a curious thing is human consciousness, that people around the globe all see the same color when they see red, but their firmly held beliefs about what happens when we die are so radically different, yet all equally fervent. Fear is the basis of all these systems of thought, wrote Bertrand Russell in his 1957 essay "Why I Am Not a Christian." Russell was born in London in 1872, went to Trinity College in Cambridge, and became a professor of mathematics there. In addition, he was widely known as a philosopher and was awarded the Nobel Prize in Literature in 1950.

One of the twentieth century's most eloquent voices of nonbelief, Russell decried the fear that he perceived as the foundation of organized religions: "Fear of the mysterious, fear of defeat, fear of death. Fear is the parent of cruelty, and therefore it is no wonder if cruelty and religion have gone hand in hand. It is because fear is at the basis of these two things. In this world we can now begin a little to understand things, and a little to master them by help of science, which has forced its way step by step against the Christian religion, against the churches, and against the operation of the old precepts. Science can help us get over this craven fear in which mankind has lived for so many generations."

Despite his background in the sciences, or perhaps because of it, Russell's optimism and faith in empiricism turned gradually to something else as the twentieth century unfolded, and in his bleaker moments he did not shy from confronting a starker reality. Even before the Great Wars, he conceded that science had little attractive to offer in the way of replacing eternal salvation for the individual person. In his essay "The Free Man's Worship," written in 1903, he pulled no punches but still found reason to celebrate the human condition:

> Even more purposeless, more void of meaning, is the world which Science presents for our belief. Amid such a world, if anywhere, our ideals henceforward must find a home. That Man is the product of causes which had no provision of the end they were

achieving; that his origin, his growth, his hopes, and fears, his loves and his beliefs, are but the outcome of accidental collocations of atoms; that no fire, no heroism, no intensity of thought and feeling, can preserve the individual life beyond the grave; that all the labors of the ages, all the devotion, all the inspiration, all the noonday brightness of the human genius, are destined to extinction. . . . All these things, if not quite beyond dispute, are yet so nearly certain that no philosophy which rejects them can hope to stand. Only within the scaffolding of these truths, only on the firm foundation of unyielding despair, can the soul's habitation henceforth be safely built. . . .

Man is yet free, during his brief years, to examine, to criticize, to know, and in imagination to create. To him alone, in the world with which he is acquainted, this freedom belongs; and in this lies his superiority to the resistless forces that control his outward life.

What conclusions have I drawn from all this reading and interviewing and thinking about immortality? That's the question my mother asked me, a month before she lay down to die, when I was deep in my research. Regretably, I had to raise my eyebrows, shrug my shoulders, shake my head, and say that so far I had not learned a thing, not one single certain thing about what happens after death. Unfortunately, now that the book is finished (and my mother is gone), this is still the case. The only thing that has changed is that I have come to believe that death is not the opposite of life; it is the opposite of birth. Our forms and those of a hundred billion like us rise and fall. Life is like the air in which we live and die; it endures even if we do not. Of course, that is of little consolation to those of us who want to hold on indefinitely to this life, this form, these loved ones, those who fear oblivion or, worse yet, a postmortem judgment.

Never mind, never mind. The other conclusion one can draw after exploring the many ways that people have constructed to think about what comes after death is that doing so is pretty much a waste of time. In the Confucian Analects, Jilu asks about the service of ghosts and spirits. Confucius answers, "You have never been able to serve people. On what basis would you serve ghosts?" Then Jilu grows even bolder: "I venture to ask about death." Confucius replied, "You have never understood life. On what basis would you understand death?"

Or, as the Buddhist masters are often quoted as asking, "Why do you want to know what will happen to you after you die? Find out who you are now!"

If we do not live forever, if this is our one passage, if nothing individual lasts, then what should we do with this, our only life? How shall we spend it? Are we born to grasp what we can, looking for maximum enjoyment? Or are we here to take part in a concerted effort among our kind to improve the world for humans and all animals, ever so slowly to evolve beyond the brute nature we know all too well, to stop causing suffering, engendering misery, spilling blood, taking lives? Or perhaps we are here for no reason at all other than to propagate our species, to keep the world turning for one more sun-to-sun. All of us move through our lives toward death. Each and every one of us, in a mud hut or a mansion, is alive and wanting to stay that way, shot through with yearnings for immortality.

BIBLIOGRAPHY

Addison, James Thayer. *Life Beyond Death: In the Beliefs of Mankind.* Boston: Houghton Mifflin, 1932.

Bowker, John. *The Meanings of Death.* Cambridge, UK: Cambridge University Press, 1991.

Brenner, Jon. *The Rise and Fall of the Afterlife.* London: Routledge, 2002.

Coward, Harold, ed. *Life after Death in World Religions.* Maryknoll, NY: Orbis, 1997.

Edwards, David. *After Death? Past Beliefs and Real Possibilities.* London: Cassell, 1999.

Flew, Anthony, ed. *Body, Mind, and Death.* New York: MacMillan, 1964.

Gallup, George, Jr., and D. Michael Lindsey. *Surveying the Religious Landscape.* New York: Moorehouse, 2000.

Gallup, George, Jr., with William Proctor. *Adventures in Immortality.* New York: McGraw-Hill, 1982.

Gruman, Gerald. *A History of Ideas about the Prolongation of Life.* New York: Springer, 2003.

Hick, John. *Death and Eternal Life.* London: MacMillan Press, 1985.

Johnson, Christopher Jay, and Marsha McGee, eds. *How Different Religions View Death and Afterlife.* Philadelphia: Charles Press, 1998.

Neusner, Jacob. *Death and the Afterlife.* Cleveland, OH: Pilgrim, 2000.

Obayashi Hiroshi, ed. *Death and Afterlife: Perspectives of World Religions.* New York: Praeger, 1992.

Patterson, A. Seth Pringle. *The Idea of Immortality.* Oxford: Oxford University Press, 1922.

Renard, John. *The Handy Religion Answer Book.* Detroit: Visible Ink, 2001.

Terkel, Studs. *Will the Circle Be Unbroken? Refletions on Death, Rebirth, and Hunger for a Faith.* New York: Ballantine, 2002.

CHAPTER 1

Blacker, Carmen, and Michael Loewe, eds. *Ancient Cosmologies.* London: George Allen & Unwin, 1975.

Boyce, Mary. *Zoroastrians: Their Religious Beliefs and Practices.* London: Routledge and Kegan Paul, 1979.

Brandon, S. G. F. *The Judgement of the Dead: An Historical and Comparative Study of the Idea of a Post-Mortem Judgement in the Major Religions.* London: Weidenfeld & Nicholson, 1967.

Budge, E. A. Wallis. *Egyptian Ideas of the Future Life.* London: Kegan Paul, Trench, Trubner, 1899.

Cohn, Norman. *The Ancient Roots of Apoalyptic Faith.* New Haven, CT: Yale University Press, 1995.

Dalley, Stephanie, trans. and ed. *Myths from Mesopotamia: Creation, the Flood, Gilgamesh, and Others.* Oxford: Oxford University Press, 1989.

Davies, Jon. *Death, Burial and Rebirth in the Religions of Antiquity.* London: Routledge, 1999.

Herodotus. *The History of Herodotus.* Trans. George Rawlinson. Chicago: Encyclopædia Britannica, 1952.

Irani, K. D., ed. *The Gathas.* Newton, MA: Center for Ancient Iranian Studies, 1998.

McDannell, Colleen, and Bernhard Lang. *Heaven: A History.* New Haven, CT: Yale University Press, 2001.

Mehr, Farang. *The Zoroastrian Tradition: An Introduction to the Ancient Wisdom of Zarathustra.* Costa Mesa, CA: Mazda, 2003.

———"'Acceptance' and 'Interfaith Marriage.'" *Humata,* Spring 1998.

Moore, Clifford Hershel. *Ancient Beliefs in the Immortality of the Soul.* New York: Longmans, Green and Co., 1931.

North, Helen. "Death and Afterlife in Greek Tragedy and Plato." In *Death and Afterlife,* ed. Hiroshi Obayashi. New York: Praeger, 1992.

Pringle, Heather. *The Mummy Congress.* London: Fourth Estate, 2002.

Radin, Paul. *Primitive Man as a Philosopher.* Rev. ed. New York: Dover, 1957.

Saggs, H. W. F. *Civilization Before Greece and Rome.* New Haven, CT: Yale University Press, 1991.

Segal, Alan. *Life After Death.* New York: Doubleday, 2004.

Spencer, A. J. *Death in Ancient Egypt.* Hammondswoth, Middlesex, UK: Penguin, 1982.

Tugwell, Simon. *Human Immortality and the Redemption of Death.* London: Darton, Longman & Todd, 1990.

West, E. W., trans. "Bundashin." In *Sacred Books of the East,* vol. 5. Oxford: Oxford University Press, 1897.

CHAPTER 2

Alcor Life Extension Foundation. www.alcor.org.

Amelang, James, ed. *A Journal of the Plague Year.* New York: Oxford University Press, 1991.

Badham, Paul. *Christian Beliefs About Life After Death.* London: MacMillan, 1976.

Badham, Paul, and Linda. *Immortality or Extinction?* Totowa, NJ: Barnes & Noble, 1982.

Bahiocchi, Samuele. *Immortality or Resurrection? A Biblical Study on Human Nature and Destiny.* Berrien Springs, MI: Biblical Perspectives, 1997.

Bova, Ben. *Immortality: How Science Is Extending Your Life Span—and Changing the World.* New York: Avon, 1998.

Chadwick, Owen. *The Secularization of the European Mind in the 19th Century.* Cambridge, UK: Cambridge University Press, 1975.

Collins, John, and Michael Fishbane, eds. *Death, Ecstasy, and Other Worldly Journeys.* Albany, NY: State University of New York Press, 1995.

Craze, Richard. *An Illustrated History of the Netherworld.* Berkeley, CA: Conari, 1996.

Cryonics Institute, www.cryonics.org.

Ettinger, Robert. *The Prospect of Immortality.* Palo Alto, CA: Ria University Press, 2005.

Fernández Olmos, Margarite, and Lizabeth Paravisini-Gebert. *Creole Religions of the Caribbean.* New York: New York University Press, 2003.

Finucane, Ronald. *Soldiers of the Faith: Crusaders and Moslems at War.* New York: St. Martin's, 1983.

Fortman, Edmund. *Everlasting Life After Death.* New York: Alba House, 1976.

Goldenberg, Robert. "Bound up in the Bond of Life: Death and Afterlife in the Jewish Tradition." In *Death and Afterlife*, ed. Hiroshi Obayashi. New York: Praeger, 1992.

Hall, Stephen. *Merchants of Immortality: Chasing the Dream of Human Life Extension*. Boston: Houghton Mifflin, 2003.

Harrington, Alan. *The Immortalist: An Approach to the Engineering of Man's Divinity*. Frogmore, St. Albans, UK: Panther, 1973.

Keck, Leander. "Death and Afterlife in the New Testament" In *Death and Afterlife*, ed. Hiroshi Obayashi. New York: Praeger, 1992.

Kelsey, Morton. *The Christian and the Supernatural*. Minneapolis: Augsburg, 1976.

Lewis, James. *Doomsday Prophecies: A Complete Guide to the End of the World*. Amherst, NY: Prometheus, 1999.

McDannell, Colleen and Bernard Lang. *Heaven: A History*. New Haven, CT: Yale University Press, 2001.

McDougall, Duncan. "The Soul: Hypothesis Concerning Soul Substance Together with Experimental Evidence of the Existence of Such Substance." *American Medicine*, April 1907.

McManners, John. *Death and the Enlightenment*. New York: Oxford University Press, 1981.

Mills, Liston, ed. *Perspectives on Death*. Nashville: Abingdon, 1969.

Obayashi, Hiroshi. "Death and Eternal Life in Christianity." In *Death and Afterlife*, ed. Hiroshi Obayashi. New York: Praeger, 1992.

Penelhum, Terence. "Christianity." In *Life After Death in World Religions*, ed. Harold Coward. Maryknoll, NY: Orbis, 1997.

Pieper, Josef. *Death and Immortality*. New York: Herder and Herder, 1969.

Pinson, DovBer. *Reincarnation and Judaism: The Journey of the Soul*. Northvale, NJ: Jason Aronson, 1999.

Raphael, Simcha Paull. *Jewish Views of the Afterlife*. Northvale, NJ: Jason Aronson, 1994.

Reicherbach, Bruce. *Is Man the Phoenix? A Study of Immortality*. Washington, DC: Christian University Press, 1978.

Reimar, Jack, ed. *Wrestling with the Angel*. New York: Schocken, 1995.

Robinson, B. A. "Druse, Druze, Mowahhidoon." www.religioustolerance.org.

Segal, Alan. *Life After Death*. New York: Doubleday, 2004.

Segerberg, Osborn Jr. *The Immortality Factor*. Toronto: Clarke, Irwin & Co, 1974.

Shibles, Warren. *Death: An Interdisciplinary Analysis.* Whitewater, WI: Language Press, 1974.

Snopes.com "Soul Man." www.snopes.com/religion/soulweight.asp.

Spillane, Jack. "Local Cryogenics Expert Sees Folly in Idea of Resurrection." *Standard-Times* (New Bedford, MA), July 9, 2002, A-1.

Stern, Chaim, ed. *Gates of Prayer for Shabbat and Weekdays.* New York: Central Conference of American Rabbis, 1994.

Stimmel, Howard Lincoln. *Rendezvous with Eternity.* New York: Abingdon-Cokesbury, 1947.

Thornton, Ted. "The Crusades, 1095–1291." www.nmhschool.org/thornton/mehistory/database/crusades.htm.

Tipler, Frank. *The Physics of Immortality.* New York: Doubleday, 1994.

Unamuno, Miguel de. *The Tragic Sense of Life in Men and Nations.* Princeton, NJ: Princeton University Press, 1972.

Weatherfield, Leslie. *After Death: A Popular Statement of the Modern Christian View of Life beyond the Grave.* New York: Abingdon-Cokesbury, 1936.

Wessinger, Catherine, ed. *Millenialism, Persecution and Violence: Historical Cases.* Syracuse, NY: Syracuse University Press, 2000.

—— *How the Millennium Comes Violently: From Jonestown to Heaven's Gate.* New York: Seven Bridges, 2000.

Wilkinson, Alec. "The Cryonic Castle." *The New Yorker,* January 19, 2004.

CHAPTER 3

Aitken, Robert. *Taking the Path of Zen.* San Francisco: North Point, 1982.

Arbuckle, Gary. "Chinese Religions" *In Life After Death in World Religions,* ed. Harold Coward. Maryknoll, NY: Orbis, 1997.

Baynes, Cary, ed. *I Ching: The Book of Changes* (Richard Wilhelm's German translation). Princeton, NJ: Bollingen, 1967.

Bjerkan, Lise. "Faces of a Saddhu: Encounters with Hindu Renouncers in Northern India." Unpublished doctoral thesis. Trondheim: Norwegian University of Science and Technology, 2005.

Blofeld, John. *Taoism: The Road to Immortality.* Boulder, CO: Shambala, 1978.

Brando, S.G.F. *The Judgement of the Dead: The Idea of Life After Death in the Major Religions.* New York, Scribner, 1967.

Chatwin, Bruce. *The Songlines*. New York: Penguin, 1988.

Eck, Diana. *Banaras: City of Light*. Princeton, NJ: Princeton University Press,

Ferm, Vergilius, ed. *An Encyclopedia of Religion*. 1945. Repr. New York: Philosophical Library, 1962.

Gómez, Miguel Andrea. *A Pilgrimage to Kashi*. Varanasi, India: Indica, 1999.

Hoffmann, Yoel, ed. *Japanese Death Poems: Written by Zen Monks and Haiku Poets on the Verge of Death*. Rutland, VT: Charles Tuttle, 1986.

Justice, Christopher. *Dying the Good Death*. Delhi, India: Sri Satguru, 1997.

Kapleau, Phillip, ed. *The Wheel of Death*. New York: Harper & Row, 1971.

———. *The Three Pillars of Zen: Teaching, Practice and Enlightenment*. New York: Anchor, 1980.

Klein, Anne. "Buddhism." In *How Different Religions View Death and the Afterlife*. Philadelphia: Charles Press, 1998.

Kohn, Livia, ed. *The Taoist Experience: An Anthology*. Albany, NY: State University of New York Press, 1993.

Mackenzie, Vicki. *Cave in the Snow*. London: Bloomsbury, 1998.

Merton, Thomas. *The Asian Journal of Thomas Merton*. New York: New Directions, 1975.

———. *Zen and the Birds of Appetite*. New York: New Directions, 1968.

———. *Mystics and Zen Masters*. New York: Dell, 1961.

Mishra, Pankaj. *An End to Suffering: The Buddha in the World*. New York: Farrar, Strauss and Giroux, 2004.

Neumaier-Dargyay, Eva. "Buddhism." In *Life After Death in World Religions*, ed. Harold Coward. Maryknoll, NY: Orbis, 1997.

Parry, Jonathan. *Death in Banaras*. Cambridge, UK: Cambridge University Press, 1994.

Pinson, Dovber. *Reincarnation and Judaism: The Journey of the Soul*. Northvale, NJ: Jason Aranson, Inc., 1999.

Prabhavananda, Swami. *The Spiritual Heritage of India*. Mylapore, Chennai, India: Sri Ramakrishna Math, 2003.

Radhakrishnan, S. *Indian Philiosophy*. Oxford: Oxford University Press, 1999.

Ram Dass. *Still Here*. New York: Riverhead, 2000.

Schmidt, Carl, ed. *Pistis Sophia.* Leiden: E. J. Brill, 1978.

Shroder, Tom. *Old Souls: The Scientific Evidence for Past Lives.* New York: Simon and Schuster, 1999.

Singh, Rana P. B. *Cultural Landscapes and the Lifeworld: Literary Images of Banaras.* Varanasi, India: Indica, 2004.

Stewart, James. *Swami Abhishiktananda: His Life Told Through His Letters.* Delhi, India: Abhishiktananda Society, 1995.

Subias, Anthony. www.antinopolis.org.

Xinzhong Yao. *An Introduction to Confucianism.* Cambridge, UK: Cambridge University Press, 2000.

Yutang, Lin, ed. *The Wisdom of Laotse.* New York: Random House, 1948.

Zaleski, Carol, and Phillip Zaleski, eds. *The Book of Heaven.* New York: Oxford University Press, 2000.

CHAPTER 4

Beattie, Rich. "A Town Where the Spirit World Rules." www.nytimes.com, July 8, 2005.

Benecke, Mark. *The Dream of Eternal Life: Biomedicine, Aging, and Immortality.* New York: Columbia University Press, 2002.

Blackmore, Susan. *In Search of the Light: The Adventures of a Parapsychologist.* Amherst, NY: Prometheus, 1996.

Bloom, Harold. *Omens of Millennium.* New York: Putnam, 1996.

Brennan, Herbie. *Death: The Great Mystery of Life.* New York: Carroll & Graf, 2002.

Brown, Fred, and Jeannie McDonald. *The Serpent Handlers: Three Families and Their Faith.* Winston Salem, NC: John F. Blair, 2000.

Burton, Thomas. *Serpent-Handling Believers.* Knoxville, TN: University of Tennessee Press, 1993.

Chatwin, Bruce. *The Songlines.* New York: Penguin, 1988.

Chopra, Deepak. *Ageless Body, Timeless Mind: The Quantum Alternative to Growing Old.* New York: Harmony, 1993.

Cohen, Daniel. *The Mysteries of Reincarnation.* New York: Dodd, Mead & Co., 1975.

Covington, Dennis. *Salvation on Sand Mountain: Snake Handling and Redemption in Southern Appalachia.* Reading, MA: Addison-Wesley, 1995.

Edward, John. *Answers from the Other Side.* New York: Princess, 2003.

Edwards, Paul. *Reincarnation: A Critical Examination*. Amherst, NY: Prometheus, 1996.

Fox, Mark. *Religion, Spirituality and the Near-Death Experience*. London: Routledge, 2003.

Frohock, Fred. *Lives of the Psychics: The Shared Worlds of Science and Mysticism*. Chicago: University of Chicago Press, 2000.

González-Wippler, Migene. *What Happens after Death: Scientific and Personal Evidence for Survival*. St. Paul, MN: Llewellyn, 1997.

Gordon, Henry. *Channeling into the New Age*. Amherst, NY: Prometheus, 1988.

Handler, Russell. *Understanding the New Age*. Grand Rapids, MI: Zondervan, 1993.

Keene, M. Lamar. *The Psychic Mafia*. Amherst, NY: Prometheus, 1997.

Kelsey, Morton. *Afterlife: The Other Side of Dying*. New York: Crossroads, 1979.

Kübler-Ross, Elisabeth. *On Death and Dying*. Repr. New York: Touchstone, 1969.

Mears, Daniel, and Christopher Ellison. "Who Buys New Age Materials? Exploring Sociodemographic, Religious, Network, and Contextual Correlates of New Age Consumption." *Sociology of Religion*, Fall 2000.

Melton, J. Gordon. "Beyond Millennialism: The New Age Transformed." Paper presented at the Institut Oecumenique, Celigny Switzerland, 2000.

———. *New Age Encyclopedia*. Detroit: Gale Research, 1990.

Moody, Raymond, Jr. *Life After Life*. Marietta, GA: Mockingbird, 1975.

Moody, Raymond, Jr. with Paul Perry. *Reunions: Visionary Encounters with Departed Loved Ones*. New York: Random House, 1993.

Pike, James. *The Other Side: An Account of My Experiences with Psychic Phenomena*. New York: Doubleday, 1968.

Roach, Mary. *Spook: Science Tackles the Afterlife*. New York: W. W. Norton, 2005.

Rawlings, Maurice. *To Hell and Back*. Nashville, TN: Thomas Nelson, 1993.

Sanford, John. *Soul Journey: A Jungian Analyst Looks at Reincarnation*. New York: Crossroads, 1991.

Schwartz, Gary. *The Afterlife Experiments: Breakthrough Scientific Evidence of Life after Death*. New York: Atria, 2002.

Wild, Russell. "Yoga, Inc." *Yoga Journal*, November 2002.

Wilson, Colin. *Survival of the Soul*. St. Paul, MN: Llewellyn, 1999.

Zaleski, Carol. "Death and Near-Death Today." In *Death, Ecstasy, and Other Worldly Journeys*, ed. John Collins and Michael Fishbane. New York: State University of New York Press, 1995.

Zukav, Gary, and Linda Francis. *The Heart of the Soul*. New York: Free Press, 2002.

CHAPTER 5

Aylmer, G. E. "Unbelief in Seventeenth-Century England." In *Puritans and Revolutionaries: Essays in Seventeenth-Century History Presented to Christopher Hill*, ed. Donald Pennington and Keith Thomas. Oxford: Oxford University Press, 1978.

Barrett, William. *Death of the Soul: From Descartes to the Computer*. New York: Anchor, 1987.

Ceronetti, Guido. *The Silence of the Body: Materials for the Study of Medicine*. New York: Farrar, Strauss and Giroux, 1993.

Chattopadhyaya, Debiprasad, ed. *Caravaka/Lokayata: An Anthology of Source Materials and Some Recent Studies*. New Delhi, India: Indian Council of Philosophical Research, 1990.

———*In Defence of Materialism in Ancient India: A Study in Caravaka/Lokayata*. New Delhi, India: People's, 1989.

Davidson, Nicholas. "Atheism in Italy, 1500–1700." In *Atheism from the Reformation to the Enlightenment*, ed. Michael Hunter and David Wootton. Oxford: Clarendon Press, 1992.

Devaraja, N. K. *Humanism in Indian Thought*. New Delhi, India: Indus, 1988.

Drachman, Anders Bjorn. *Atheism in Pagan Antiquity*. London: Gylendal, 1922.

Dzielska, Maria. *Hypatia of Alexandria*. Cambridge, MA: Harvard University Press, 1995.

Freud, Sigmund. *The Future of an Illusion*. New York: W. W. Norton, 1961.

———. "Thoughts on War and Death." In *Collected Papers*, vol. 4. New York: Basic, 1959.

———. *The Standard Edition of the Complete Psychological Works of Sigmund Freud*, vol. 14. London: Hogarth, 1957.

Ginzburg, Carlo. *El queso y los gusanos* (*The Worm and the Cheese*). Barcelona, Spain: Muchnik Editores, 1994.

Grigsby, Bryon. "Medical Misconceptions." www.the-orb.net/non_spec./ missteps/ch4.html.

Harbour, Daniel. *An Intelligent Person's Guide to Atheism*. London: Gerald Duckworth, 2001.

Hill, Christopher. *The World Turned Upside Down*. London: Temple Smith, 1972.

Hunter, Michael, and David Wootton, eds. *Atheism from the Reformation to the Enlightenment*. Oxford: Clarendon, 1992.

Israel, Jonathan. *Radical Enlightenment*. Oxford: Oxford University Press, 2001.

Jacoby, Susan. *Freethinkers: A History of American Secularism*. New York: Henry Holt, 2004.

Joshi, S. T., ed. *Atheism: A Reader*. Amherst, NY: Prometheus, 2000.

Kessler, John. "Giordano Bruno: The Forgotten Philosopher." www.positiveatheism.org/hist/bruno.htm.

Landman, Howard. "Hypatia of Alexandria." www.polyamory.org/ howard/Hypatia.

Mittal, Kewel Krishan. *Materialism in Indian Thought*. New Delhi, India: Munshiram Manoharial, 1974.

Pennington, Donald, and Keith Thomas, eds. *Puritans and Revolutionaries: Essays in Seventeenth-Century History Presented to Christopher Hill*. Oxford: Oxford University Press, 1978.

Ramachandra Rao, Goporaju. *An Aetheist with Ghandi*. Ahmedabad, India: Navajivan, 1986.

Rhys Davids, T. W., trans. *The Dialogues of the Buddha*. London: H. Frowde, Oxford University Press, 1899.

Smart, J. J. C., and J. J. Haldane. *Atheism and Theism*. Oxford: Blackwell, 1997.

Thomas, Keith. *Religion and the Decline of Magic*. London: Penguin, 1973.

Thrower, James. *Western Atheism: A Short History*. Amherst, NY: Prometheus, 2000.

Wootton, David. "New Histories of Atheism." In *Atheism from the Reformation to the Enlightenment*, ed. Michael Hunter and David Wootton. Oxford: Clarendon, 1992.

CHAPTER 6

Bavidge, Michael, and Ian Ground. *Can We Understand Animal Minds?* London: Bristol Classical, 1994.

Blackmore, Susan. *Consciousness: An Introduction.* Abingdon, UK: Hodder & Stoughton, 2003.

Budiansky, Stephen. *If a Lion Could Talk: Animal Intelligence and the Evolution of Consciousness.* New York: Free Press, 1998.

Crick, Francis. *The Astonishing Hypothesis: The Scientific Search for the Soul.* New York: Charles Scribner's Sons, 1994.

Dawkins, Marian Stamp. *Through Our Eyes Only: The Search for Animal Consciousness.* Oxford: Oxford University Press, 1998.

Dean, Cornelia. "Scientists Speak up on God and Science." *The New York Times,* August 27, 2005, www.nytimes.com.

Dennett, Daniel. *Kinds of Minds: Toward an Understanding of Consciousness.* New York: Basic, 1996.

Griffin, Donald. *Animal Minds.* Chicago: University of Chicago Press, 1992.

Hawking, Stephen. *A Brief History of Time: From the Big Bang to Black Holes.* New York: Bantam, 1988.

Jibu, Mari, and Kunio Yasue. *Quantum Brain Dynamics and Consciousness: An Introduction.* Amsterdam: John Benjamins, 1995.

Johnson, George. *Fire in the Mind: Science, Faith and the Search for Order.* New York: Penguin, 1997.

Koch, Christof. *The Quest for Consciousness: A Neurobiological Approach.* Englewood, CO: Roberts & Company, 2004.

Lamont, Corliss. *The Illusion of Immortality.* New York: Philosophical Library, 1950.

Lodge, Oliver. "The Possibility of Survival from a Scientific Point of View." In *Phantom Walls.* London: Hodder & Stoughton, 1929.

McGinn, Colin. *The Mysterious Flame: Conscious Minds in a Material World.* New York: Basic, 2000.

Roebuck, John. Letter to the author about animals and heaven. October 10, 2005.

Russell, Bertrand. *The Basic Writings of Bertrand Russell: 1903–1959.* New York: Simon and Schuster, 1961.

———. *Russell on Religion: Selections from the Writings of Bertrand Russell.* London: Routledge, 1999.

Sanchís, Ima. "En nosotros hay células immortales." *La Vanguardia*, September 10, 2005, p. 76.

Wade, Nicholas. *A Natural History of Vision*. Cambridge, MA: Massachusetts Institute of Technology Press, 1998.

Wertheim, Margaret. "After the Double Helix: Unraveling the Mysteries of the State of Being." *The New York Times*, April 13, 2004.

INDEX

Note: page numbers in *italics* refer to illustrations

Index

Banaras. *See* Varanasi, India (formerly
Banaras or Kashi)
Barcelona, Spain
atheism in, 224–25
plague in, 76–77
as research center, 231–34, 245–47
Roman Catholicism in, 131–34,
224
Bedford, James, 45
behaviorism, 244
Benecke, Mark, 156–57, 158
Bhagavad Gita (sacred literature), 92,
143
Bible
heaven in, 83
resurrection in, 57, 64–65, 71–72
snake handling and, 181
valley of bones in, 21
Binhazim, Awadh, 81–83
Bloom, Harold, 158, 160–61, 162
Bodhidharma, 111
bodies, dead. *See* corpses; funerary prac-
tices
body, new or spiritual, 65–68, 71–72,
133
Bogart, Mary, 176–78
bonobos, 245, 246
Book of Going Forth by Day, The, 18–19
"Book of Life," 57, 81
Bosch, Hieronymous, *40*
Bova, Ben, 53
Boyce, Mary, 20, 23
Boyle, Robert, 51, 215
Brahma (deity), 109–10
Brahmanism. *See* Hinduism
Brahmins, Lokayata criticism of, 192
brain research, 236–41
Brandon, S. G. F., 135–36, 137
Brennan, Herbie, 171, 172
Brenner, Jon, 158–59
Breughel the Elder, *40*
Brhaspati, 192
Brhaspati sutra, 192–93
British Society for Psychical Research,
171, 173, 236
Broca, Pierre, 237

Brown-Séquard, Charles Edouard, 52
Bruno, Giordano, 208
Buddha, the (Siddartha Gautama), 109,
110–11
Buddhism
basic concepts, 109–10
branches of, 111–15
compassion in, 124
dissolution of soul in, 134
in Nashville, 115–17
Siddartha Gautama and, 110–11
Taoism and, 139
Western religions and, 141–43,
144–45
Budge, E. A. Wallis, 14–15
Bundahishn (sacred literature), 23–24
burial, 17, 27. *See also* funerary
practices
Burton, Thomas, 182
business of religion
Christianity, 168–69
Hinduism in Varanasi, India, 96–97,
101–3
New Age movement, 160–61, 168
psychics and mediums, 169–72,
175–79

C
Canuove, Commodo, 209–10
Cardano, Gerolamo, 210
Carnes, Bruce, 54–55
Caron, Alexandre, *2*
Carpocrates, 123, 124–26
Carpocratians, 123–26
Carroll, Lee, 166
Cartesianism, 213–14
Carvaka, 193
Catalan government and Catholic
Church, 232. *See also* Barcelona,
Spain
Catalan Institute for Research and
Advanced Studies, 231–32
Cave in the Snow (Thurman), 144–45
cell death, 53–54
Celts, 121
Ch'an Buddhism, 111

Index

Index

Index

Index

ACKNOWLEDGMENTS

Immortality is not an easy subject to consider, and in order to embark on this project I interviewed a number of people who do not appear in the book but whose thoughts on the subject contributed greatly to the final product. Any errors are my own, but their kindness in granting me their time was a big help, and I give deep thanks to Nashvillians Devang Bhatt, Teddy Bart, James Brewer, Dan Canale, Sonnye Dixon, John Seigenthaler, Charles Stroebel, Gene Teselle, and Barry and Holly Tashian; and in Varanasi to Mark Dyczkowski, Uma Giri, and Rana P. B. Singh.

People helped in a number of other ways, and thanks are due for assistance rendered: José Manuel Alvárez Flores, Govinda Baba, Leopoldo Blume, Amy Calzadilla, Saul Calzadilla, John Egerton, Roger Guettinger, Susan Humphrey, Sue Katz, Alan and Andrée Le Quire, Alberto Martínez, Carmen Martínez, Silvia Omedes, Anne Paine, Oscar Pujol, Chris Ryan, Rakesh Singh, Sunny Singh, Tom Brittingham, and Vikram.